Conference on the U.N. Special Session on Disarmament, Talloires, France, 1977.

Opportunities for Disarmament

A Preview of the 1978 United Nations Special Session on Disarmament

Edited by Jane M.O. Sharp

CARNEGIE ENDOWMENT FOR INTERNATIONAL PEACE
NEW YORK   WASHINGTON, D.C.

I.S.B.N. 0-87003-011-6

Library of Congress Catalog Card Number: 77-93153

Printed in the United States of America

Contents

83564

Participants

Conference on the U.N.
Special Session on Disarmament
Talloires, France, September 1977

Sponsored by the Carnegie Endowment for
International Peace and the
Arms Control Association

Chairman: H.E. Max Jacobson, Council of Economic
Organizations, Finland

H.E. Dimce Belovski, Ambassador of Yugoslavia to U.S.A.

Dr. Francesco Calogero, University of Rome, Italy

Dr. Alessandro Corradini, Center for Disarmament,
United Nations

Dr. William Epstein, University of Victoria, Canada

Dr. Bernard T. Feld, Massachusetts Institute of Technology,
U.S.A.

Hon. Adrian Fisher, U.S. Ambassador to the Conference of the
Committee on Disarmament

H.E. C.R. Gharekan, Permanent Representative of India to
the U.N. in Geneva, India

Mr. Jean-Louis Gergorin, Ministry of Foreign Affairs, France

Dr. Jozef Goldblat, Political Scientist, Sweden

Mr. Jean Goormaghtigh, Centre de Recherches sur les Institutions Internationales, Switzerland

Hon. Thomas L. Hughes, Carnegie Endowment for International Peace, U.S.A.

Dr. Mary Kaldor, University of Sussex, Great Britain

Dr. Martin Kaplan, Pugwash, Switzerland

Dr. Ashok Kapur, University of Waterloo, Canada

Mr. Andrzej Karkoszka, Polish Institute of International Affairs, Poland

H.E. Arthur Lall, India

Dr. Betty Goetz Lall, Cornell University, U.S.A.

Mr. Miguel Marin, Delegation of Mexico to the Conference of the Committee on Disarmament

Dr. Robert Nield, University of Cambridge, Great Britain

H.E. Motoo Ogiso, Permanent Representative of Japan to the Conference of the Committee on Disarmament

Dr. Andrew Pierre, Council on Foreign Relations, U.S.A.

Mr. Jan Prawitz, Ministry of Defense, Sweden

Ms. Enid C.B. Schoettle, Ford Foundation, U.S.A.

Dr. Herbert Scoville, Jr., Arms Control Association, U.S.A.

Prof. Jean Siotis, Graduate School of International Studies, Switzerland

---

Consultant: Macha DeG. Levinson, Switzerland

Rapporteur: Jane M.O. Sharp, Program for Science and International Affairs, Harvard University, U.S.A.

Foreword

Some years ago, in a spirit of both hope and promise, the United Nations declared the period 1970 to 1980 to be the "disarmament decade." Events since then have met the expectations of neither the cynics nor the idealists. Amid new and renewed conflicts, there have been significant steps toward a world less shaped and dominated by the instruments of war. As the decade nears its end, therefore, it is appropriate to take stock of the gains and losses, to divine their meanings for the course of international security, and to make proposals for future activity.

In terms of the sheer number of arms control agreements concluded, the 1970s must be viewed as fruitful in comparison to any other period in modern history. Among these accords are the 1971 treaty banning weapons of mass destruction on the seabed; the agreements signed by the United States and the Soviet Union in the same year to reduce the risk of nuclear war and to improve the Moscow-Washington "hotline"; the 1972 convention prohibiting the development, production and stockpiling of bacteriological and toxin weapons; the Anti-Ballistic Missile Treaty and the Interim Offensive Weapons Agreement, concluded by the United States and the Soviet Union in 1972 and known collectively as SALT I; and the 1977 convention banning the military or hostile use of environmental modification techniques. Added to the accords of the prior decade (the Antarctic Treaty, the original "hotline" agreement, the Limited Test Ban Treaty, the Outer Space Treaty, the Treaty of Tlatelolco for the Prohibition of Nuclear Weapons in Latin America, and the Non-Proliferation Treaty), these agreements constitute an impressive record.

Compared to the pace of technological innovation, however, these steps have fallen short. A comprehensive ban on nuclear testing still has to be concluded fifteen years after the framers of the limited test ban undertook to achieve the discontinuance of all test explosions of nuclear weapons. No practical progress has been made in regard to the production and international traffic in conventional arms. Still on the negotiating agenda and complicated by new technological possibilities are a new accord on offensive strategic weapons (SALT II) and the problem of chemical warfare, itself the subject of another publication by the Carnegie Endowment, *Chemical Weapons and Chemical Arms Control.* At the same time, modern technology has begun to threaten the regimes established under the Non-Proliferation Treaty and the Outer Space Treaty, suggesting that supplementary steps must be taken to limit or otherwise take account of technological developments which could only be dimly foreseen when these agreements were concluded.

Finally, while satisfaction can be taken from the fact that the parties to the agreements thus far concluded have observed and honored their pledges, many states remain outside their provisions. Likewise, many of the agreements so far developed were produced by, and often limited to, the United States and the Soviet Union, with other nations remaining outside the process of arms control negotiation.

In response to perceived shortcomings in arms control efforts, and largely at the initiative of the group of non-aligned countries, the U.N. General Assembly voted to convene a Special Session on Disarmament in May, 1978. As a contribution to preparations for this enterprise, the Carnegie Endowment and the Arms Control Association held an informal "preview" conference of international experts in Talloires, France, in September, 1977. Under the chairmanship of Ambassador Max Jakobson of Finland, who chaired the Endowment's 1974 preview of the Non-Proliferation Treaty Review Conference, twenty-six experts from over a dozen countries, as well as from the United Nations and other international organizations, met to discuss the major problems of disarmament and possible solutions for them.

As with past conferences of this type, papers were prepared in advance by some of the participants for discussion at Talloires. These papers and a summary of the principal elements of the discussion, as well as a selected bibliography and the texts of pertinent treaties, resolutions and statements, are brought together in this volume. The working papers are published as modified after the discussions at Talloires, while the conference report, which summarizes the discussions themselves, was prepared by the conference secretariat based on comments made by participants on a draft report at the conference's final plenary session.

Taken together, the discussion papers and the conference summary also provide an agenda of the most pressing problems in arms control and disarmament and a number of recommendations for action in the near future, both within and beyond the framework of the Special Session, including organizational initiatives. Recognizing that reversing the course of arms races requires unilateral restraint, painstaking bilateral or multilateral negotiations, and international diplomatic efforts to improve global security, the participants in the Talloires discussions agreed that the Special Session on Disarmament provides a singular opportunity to spur concrete steps toward nuclear arms control, to pursue discussions on the limitation of conventional weaponry and to develop innovative approaches which will involve more governments in the urgent problems of arms control and disarmament.

It is hoped that publication of this volume will help to clarify the primary issues bearing on the Special Session, both for the delegates and for the wider public. As always, Endowment sponsorship of the report implies only a belief in the importance of the subject. The report is not intended to reflect, and does not reflect, the unanimous views of participants, none of whom has signed the text. Nor can it be taken to represent the view of any government or institution with which particular participants are identified, since all participants attended the conference solely in their private capacities.

The sponsoring organizations express their appreciation to the Ford Foundation for its generous financial assistance.

Thomas A. Halsted, former executive director of the Arms Control Association, conceived and organized the Talloires conference and Herbert Scoville, Jr., vice president of the Arms Control Association, served as conference director. Macha DeG. Levinson served as consultant to the conference and Jane M.O. Sharp as conference rapporteur and editor of this volume.

Comments or inquiries on this and other publications of the Endowment are welcomed and may be addressed to the Carnegie Endowment for International Peace, 345 East 46th Street, New York City 10017 or 11 Dupont Circle, N.W., Washington, D.C. 20036.

Thomas L. Hughes, President   Archibald S. Alexander,
Carnegie Endowment   President
for International Peace   The Arms Control Association

U.N. Special Session on Disarmament

Preview of the Issues

In December, 1976, the General Assembly of the United Nations decided that a Special Session on Disarmament (UNSSOD) should be held in May and June, 1978.

The participants in the Talloires preview conference agreed that the Special Session was most timely in view of the recent acceleration in both nuclear and conventional arms races, which is producing economic and social burdens on rich and poor alike without increasing the security of any. Arms control and disarmament negotiations have failed to keep pace with advancing military technology and rising levels of armaments. Nuclear arsenals of the nuclear-weapon states are larger and more dangerous than ever before, and the risks of nuclear weapons becoming available to additional governments and non-governmental groups are daily becoming greater. The size and sophistication of weapons stockpiles for conventional conflicts, which may engulf peoples in every corner of the world, are also growing at an alarming rate. The world must urgently address the question of genuine disarmament, nuclear and conventional, or face disaster.

The Special Session on Disarmament provides the opportunity for nations throughout the world to consider new approaches for stopping and reversing these arms races. Delegates should take the opportunity of a special session to examine critically the prevalent assumptions about the nature of military power which seem to underlie current arms control and other security policies. As long as political power is thought to reside in military power measured primarily in terms of armaments, effective arms limitation and disarmament remain difficult. The Special Session should encourage a new climate of opinion, in which the prospect of arms reductions does not imply a concomitant reduction in political power and international prestige and in which the relationship between disarmament and development is explicitly recognized.

The participants at the Talloires conference saw their task as assisting the delegates to the Special Session, preparatory groups, and the wider public in focusing attention on global problems of both nuclear and conventional armaments, recommending specific items for inclusion in a priority program of action for disarmament, and suggesting appropriate means for implementation.

Six papers were prepared as a basis for discussion at the conference, and the group divided its deliberations into the following three areas which relate to the proposed Program of Action for Disarmament in the draft agenda for the Special Session.

- measures to limit and reduce nuclear arms,
- measures to limit and reduce conventional arms, and
- approaches and machinery for expediting and implementing disarmament.

Measures to Limit and Reduce Nuclear Arms

The conference agreed that top priority at the Special Session on Disarmament should be accorded to the limitation and reduction of nuclear weapons stockpiles and the spread of nuclear weapons.

A halt to all nuclear testing was considered the single most important measure that could be achieved in the immediate future. A comprehensive test ban (CTB) should include all the nuclear-weapon states as well as other states, but it would still be useful if it was initially adhered to only by the United States, the U.S.S.R. and the United Kingdom. However, since the continued absence of China, France and other potential nuclear-weapon states could cause problems, a comprehensive test ban should be reviewed after an agreed number of years to see if it was still in the best security interests of all parties.

The comprehensive test ban treaty should include a moratorium on peaceful nuclear explosion (PNE) tests, since it was agreed that such tests are indistinguishable from nuclear weapons tests. The duration of the moratorium should be long enough to ensure that weapons development is halted. There was widespread concern that continued peaceful nuclear explosions, which would provide a loophole for military experiments,

2

would undermine a test ban. Some thought that if a comprehensive test ban did not specifically ban them, the number of tests designated "peaceful" would almost certainly increase.

The U.N. Special Session on Disarmament should commission expert studies to clarify the peaceful nuclear explosion problem. These should explore: the potential utility of peaceful nuclear explosions, taking into account environmental problems; the feasibility of verifying that peaceful tests are not used for military purposes; and the international mechanisms under which peaceful nuclear explosions might be authorized and conducted if and when they are considered practical.

There were other individual views on the issue. One was that a comprehensive test ban should ban all nuclear testing, making no distinction between weapons tests and peaceful explosions.

A second view was that such a ban should be both general and comprehensive, i.e., adhered to by all the nuclear-weapon states and applied to all environments; further, peaceful nuclear explosions should not be controlled in a weapons test ban but, in this view, regulated in a separate international regime to be negotiated after conclusion of a weapons test ban treaty. One rationale for this view was the precedent set by the superpowers with their negotiation of separate threshold test ban and peaceful nuclear explosion treaties.

Some participants urged that a ban on peaceful nuclear explosions might be made more acceptable if it provided for the establishment of an international authority, whose prior authorization would be required before any peaceful nuclear tests could be undertaken by any state.

Finally, a view was expressed that no comprehensive test ban can be isolated from the general problem of reducing the stockpiles of nuclear armaments and freezing their qualitative development.

Implementation of Article VI of the Non-Proliferation Treaty must begin. For the nuclear-weapon states, in addition to halting all nuclear testing, this should initially include:

- agreement to a cut-off in production of fusionable material for weapons use,
- agreement to a cut-off in production and deployment of strategic delivery vehicles and defensive systems,
- agreement not to deploy new types of nuclear weapons and delivery vehicles, and
- significant reductions in strategic nuclear weapons and delivery vehicles.

The nuclear-weapon states must provide assurances that they will not use, or threaten to use, nuclear weapons against the

3

non-nuclear-weapon states. Some participants supported declarations of no-first-use against any state by the nuclear-weapon powers, while others would only support declarations on non-use if accompanied by appropriate disarmament measures.

Steps should be taken to raise, not lower, the nuclear threshold and maintain a clear demarcation between nuclear and non-nuclear armaments. The conference endorsed the concept of nuclear-weapon-free zones on the Latin American model (Treaty of Tlatelolco), which would create obligations for the nuclear-weapon states not to station nuclear weapons on foreign territories and not to use or threaten to use nuclear weapons against states in such zones. However, it was recognized that the establishment of such zones would have to depend on the initiative of the states concerned and on the circumstances in each zone.

In view of the difficulties of regional approaches, a draft convention for the renunciation of nuclear weapons, open to all states, stimulated considerable discussion.

The current non-proliferation regime should be strengthened. Measures should include:

- assured nuclear fuel supplies and services, under effective safeguards and at equitable prices, should be guaranteed to states willing to renounce nuclear technologies which could lead to a nuclear explosive capability,
- rigorous physical security measures should be applied to protect weapons-grade fissionable material, and
- the U.N. Special Session on Disarmament should promote studies of non-nuclear alternative energy sources.

Measures to Limit and Reduce Conventional Arms

Major producers and suppliers of conventional arms, particularly the United States, the U.S.S.R., France and the United Kingdom, should take immediate steps to restrain arms sales, initiate limits on production, as well as cut back their own conventional arms stockpiles. Recipient countries should complement restraints adopted by the suppliers by establishing principles of restraint with respect to arms imports. Some of these principles might be specific to a given region, but effective limitation will be strengthened by general acceptance of guidelines for restraint.

There was a consensus that more attention should be given to the conventional weapons dimension of the arms race. The quantitative and qualitative increase in world-wide conventional arms and their significant augmentation in several regions of

4

the world poses grave risks for international security and peace. In this connection the conference welcomed the guidelines on arms transfers announced in May, 1977, by the government of the United States. Such actions by the United States could encourage similar unilateral restraints by other states and help create the right atmosphere at the U.N. Special Session on Disarmament and elsewhere to generate restraints from the other major suppliers. It might also help generate restraints in the purchase of conventional arms by recipient states.

It was stressed that the time was ripe for action in this area, with the world's largest producer and supplier of arms expressing a willingness to exercise significant restraints and before new producers have yet developed viable arms exporting industries. One participant warned that the control of conventional armaments could become unmanageable if constraints are not applied in the near future.

Any guidelines for suppliers should be drawn up in consultation with representative recipients in order to avoid any implication that major weapons-exporting nations are attempting to dictate the security requirements of the less developed nations. Some participants felt that the ability of larger nations to dictate requirements would be reduced by limitations on arms transfers, whether they were initiated by supplier or recipient nations.

Supplier restraints could best be applied through an agreement, tacit or formal, between the major countries concerned, with the hope that secondary suppliers could be persuaded to accept whatever guidelines were adopted by the primary ones.

Restrictions on arms transfers must be part of a program coupled with reductions in production and deployment of conventional armaments by the supplier countries.

The overwhelming consensus at Talloires was that the U.N. Special Session on Disarmament should consider the issue of conventional arms transfer restraints, in view of the enormous quantitative and qualitative increases in recent years and particularly the introduction of highly sophisticated weapons into areas of potential conflict. One participant dissented.

Approaches and Machinery for Expediting and Implementing Disarmament

UNILATERAL STEPS

There was general agreement that unilateral cuts and other forms of restraint in the acquisition and development of weapons were an important approach to disarmament. It was proposed that disarmament, like charity, should begin at home, and that, instead of making its actions conditional on those of others, each nation should consider whether it might announce some unilateral steps at the Special Session. In support of this view it was stressed that where states did not face any specific military threat the causes for the arms build-up were domestic and that unilateral action therefore could be taken without requiring reciprocity. Similarly, substantial cuts could be made by countries whose arsenals were excessive, with a large "overkill" capacity.

These unilateral steps could be designed to induce responses from other nations. The scope of action would vary from country to country; in some cases it might be impossible to move unilaterally.

A further possible form of action, mentioned by some as a disarmament mechanism, is the unilateral offer of an arms reduction conditional, implicitly or explicitly, on a response from one or more other nations.

It may be desirable that arms limitations resulting from moves along any of these lines be codified and made more permanent in treaties.

PUBLIC FOCUS ON DISARMAMENT

The U.N. Special Session on disarmament was widely welcomed as a way of focusing world attention on the disarmament problem and on bringing it back to the center of the concerns of the United Nations, the press and public opinion. However, it was stressed that in order to accomplish this, disarmament should be considered in the broader context of economic development. It was necessary to study the socio-economic causes of the arms race, as well as the role played by prestige and perceived military threats.

The importance of providing experts with opportunities to contribute on the basis of their independent judgment rather than as government representatives was emphasized.

Some felt that the Special Session might be more productive if governments set up study groups or commissions of scientists, scholars and representatives of non-governmental organizations to prepare new initiatives and proposals for the Special Session.

There was discussion of the importance of having increased public knowledge of disarmament negotiations, their objectives, their progress, and the difficulties encountered in bringing them to a successful conclusion.

PROGRAM OF ACTION

A number of measures to limit and reduce both nuclear and conventional arms for inclusion in a priority Program of Action are outlined above. Consideration was also given at the Talloires conference to the program of action suggested by the non-aligned states in which all the proposed measures were recognized as necessary.

Support was expressed for the development of a comprehensive program for disarmament which might include measures in order of their urgency. Emphasis was also placed on the importance of indicating the time required for the achievement of these measures.

ORGANIZATION FOR NEGOTIATIONS

There was consensus that every effort should be made to bring all the nuclear-weapon states into the disarmament negotiations. In this context the August, 1977, announcement by the French government that it had commenced work on a comprehensive disarmament plan was welcomed, and it was hoped that some restructuring of the Conference of the Committee on Disarmament (CCD) might lead to the participation of France and China.

There was some discussion of the possibility of changing the co-chairmanship of the Conference of the Committee on Disarmament to facilitate participation by other nuclear powers. The Conference should be receptive to such proposals and therefore the Special Session might consider recommending changes in the structure of the Conference, its membership, and the institution of the co-chairmanship as well. Such changes might be possible, but it would be important to know whether the other nuclear powers were ready to enter the negotiations.

One proposal for bringing all the nuclear-weapon states into the negotiations would be to implement Article 26 of the U.N. Charter, which gave the Security Council responsibility for the regulation of armaments. In this way France and China, as permanent U.N. members, would automatically be included, and the link between disarmament would be reinforced. Although it was pointed out that this approach had been tried in the past, it was thought that under present circumstances it was worthy of reconsideration.

There was consensus that the disarmament role of the United Nations should be strengthened. Suggestions included an annual report by the secretary general surveying developments in the field of armaments and disarmament, the establishment by the United Nations of a new standing arms review committee that would review the arms programs of the member states, and the holding of a U.N. Special Session on Disarmament every two or three years to assess the progress made towards disarmament.

ORGANIZATION FOR VERIFICATION

It was noted that the establishment of a multilateral consultative committee as incorporated in the recently signed Environmental Modification Treaty (ENMOD) represented a precedent in recognizing the right of all parties to a treaty to participate in verification, and that it was important to establish commissions of experts for these purposes in future arms limitation and disarmament agreements, although the actual mechanics of verification might vary from case to case.

It was pointed out during the discussions that the right of parties to verify a treaty was meaningless unless they had access to the information gathered by sophisticated technical methods which until now has been available only to a few nations. Therefore, it is important to share this information and to institute multilateral verification arrangements.

The Cessation of Nuclear Testing

Herbert Scoville, Jr.

Background

The U.N. General Assembly has perennially passed resolutions, favored by large majorities of more than 100 nations, calling for the cessation of nuclear weapons tests and the conclusion of a comprehensive test ban treaty (CTBT). Each year the nuclear-weapon states either abstain or (in the case of China) vote against these resolutions. The United Nations has been powerless in the fourteen years since the signing of the Limited Test Ban Treaty (LTBT) to exert any influence on this issue, even though most nations throughout the world consider continued testing a major threat to the future of mankind and view a commitment to halt testing as a prime indicator of the seriousness with which the nuclear-weapon nations approach nuclear disarmament.

Meanwhile nuclear explosions have continued to take place, underground on the part of the United States and the U.S.S.R. and in the atmosphere on the part of China and France. The United States conducted eighteen tests and the U.S.S.R. thirteen between January, 1976, and July, 1977, all of which were underground. The United Kingdom's nuclear program has been inconsequential since the 1963 Limited Test Ban Treaty. Most of the sixty-four French tests have been conducted in the atmosphere, though public pressure in France has induced the government to refrain from testing above ground in the past three years. India detonated one nuclear explosion underground in 1974, ostensibly for peaceful purposes, but India's new prime minister, Morarji Desai, has recently stated that India will not carry out any further explosions.[1]

Until the summer of 1977, there was virtually no progress in the negotiations to achieve a total ban on all tests. The Conference of the Committee on Disarmament, charged with responsibility in this area, has discussed this issue over the years and sponsored a number of conferences of experts to explore the major improvements in verification achieved in the last fifteen years, but an actual treaty was no closer at the beginning of 1977 than it was in 1964.

President Carter has made the cessation of all nuclear tests an important administration goal. In an attempt to break the impasse on the road to a comprehensive test ban treaty, Secretary of State Vance, during his visit to Moscow in March, 1977, laid the groundwork for the informal discussions which began in Geneva in July between representatives from the United Kingdom, the U.S.S.R., and the United States. These developed into more formal negotiations in the fall of 1977. While at this writing it is still too early to say whether any real progress has been made, hopes for a treaty are running higher in early 1978 than at any time during the previous decade.

In 1974, the United States and the U.S.S.R. began bilateral negotiations to halt at least tests of higher yield devices. These culminated in the Threshold Test Ban Treaty (TTBT), signed in 1974 by President Nixon and Secretary Brezhnev, and the Peaceful Nuclear Explosion Treaty (PNET), signed in 1976 by President Ford. As of January, 1978, neither accord had been ratified or come into force, although both nations said they would not test above the threshold (150 kilotons) during the ratification interval. Hearings in the U.S. Senate on ratification of these treaties began on July 28, 1977, and the Senate Foreign Relations Committee ordered them to be favorably reported on September 21, 1977.

Unfortunately, neither of these treaties is an important step toward, and could even be steps away from, a comprehensive ban on nuclear testing. The threshold that would be established by the treaty is so high that it stops very little that either country desires to do; furthermore, it bears no relationship to verification capabilities, which can verify nuclear explosions well below the 150 kiloton range. In signing these treaties the United States discarded the principle that it was willing to halt all tests that could be verified. Continued testing for military purposes was thus tacitly endorsed. The Peaceful Nuclear Explosion Treaty also gave new legitimacy to "peaceful" explosions by implying that they were somehow distinct from weapons tests. India and other nations have been able to point to this in defending their desire to keep open the option of developing nuclear explosives. The negotiators of the Peaceful Nuclear Explosion Treaty were forced to the conclusion, however, that peaceful explosions could not be differentiated from weapons tests for verification purposes. The elaborate procedures in the treaty for on-site inspection of multiple peaceful explosions with total yield above the threshold have little if any application to the verification of a comprehensive ban and might give credence to the claim that similar procedures were necessary for a comprehensive test ban treaty.

Issues to be Resolved to Achieve a Comprehensive Ban

VERIFICATION

Inability to agree on verification procedures has been the stated excuse for the failure to achieve a comprehensive test ban. The U.S.S.R. has claimed that national technical means are adequate, but the United States has asserted that on-site inspections of unidentified events are also needed.

In 1963 when the Limited Test Ban Treaty came into effect, seismic capabilities for differentiating between the signals from earthquakes and from explosions were quite limited. However, since then, primarily as a result of American and British research programs, the science of verification has been significantly improved, and a number of reliable criteria are now available for distinguishing between artificial and natural seismic events. When used together, these criteria provide a high probability of identifying almost all detectable earthquakes and explosions. There would now be few, if any, *unidentifiable* events, except at the low-yield borderline of detectability, i.e. a few kilotons or less. Since an event must be *detected but unidentifiable* in order to trigger any on-site inspection, the value of on-site inspection procedures has become quite limited.

Furthermore, verification has been improved by the availability of satellite photography to observe suspected test sites for signs of tests and test activity. For example, one method of raising the level of the yield of tests that might escape seismic detection (perhaps by a factor of ten) would be to explode a device in dry, soft alluvium, which could muffle the seismic signals. However, unless such an explosion is several thousand feet deep, it will leave a visible crater where dry soil above the explosion subsides into the cavity produced at the explosion depth. Satellites can easily detect such craters (the U.S. Nevada test site is pockmarked with them), and this prevents

11

such explosions from being carried out secretly. Dry alluvium is almost never found at sufficient depths to avoid such crater formation for explosions greater than a few kilotons.

Apart from testing in alluvium, a number of other methods of concealing explosions have been considered. Few have much merit. For example, placing the device in a large deep hole, perhaps 100 meters in radius, poses severe engineering problems, rendering such tactics impractical for a weapons development program. Perhaps the most feasible method might be to pre-locate the test device and prepare to fire it in the immediate aftermath of a large earthquake, when the seismic noise from the natural event had raised the detection threshold of the seismic system. Even this rather difficult procedure could be rendered more unreliable if seismic instruments could be located relatively close to possible test areas instead of a thousand or more miles away. The use of remote, unattended seismic stations has been proposed as a supplementary verification procedure. Since this would not involve intrusive activities within national borders it might be more acceptable to the Soviet Union than on-site inspections. But it is not clear that this measure is necessary.

Finally, Soviet objections to any on-site inspections have lessened in the last year or so. In a speech on March 21, 1977, Secretary Brezhnev said, in reference to a ban on nuclear testing, "in order to clear the road to agreement, it (the U.S.S.R.) is ready for on-the-spot inspections on a voluntary basis, in the event of any doubts concerning the fulfillment of treaty commitments." This had been preceded by similar remarks by Foreign Minister Gromyko at the U.N. General Assembly in September, 1976.

In the bilateral Strategic Arms Limitation agreements (SALT I) the Standing Consultative Committee (SCC) was established to discuss ambiguities which might arise with reference to the Anti-Ballistic Missile (ABM) Treaty and the Interim Agreement on Offensive Weapons. A similar but multinational commission might be established under a comprehensive test ban treaty to resolve ambiguities in seismic monitoring results.

It must be recognized, however, that some very low yield explosions could be carried out with only a slight probability of detection. As the yield or energy release goes down below the kiloton level, the number of natural events which could be confused with a test goes up rapidly. The earth is continually rumbling with seismic noise, which blanks out small explosions and makes their detection very unlikely. Governments will always have to make a political decision on whether the risks of developments rising out of possible secret, very low yield tests are greater than the risks of continued nuclear testing at all levels.

Under the kind of monitoring and verification regimes now possible, tests of all types of strategic weapons would be ruled out because their yield would be so high that they could easily be detected. The same would apply to most tactical, naval or air defense weapons. Only the very low yield tests (of devices such as the so-called "neutron" bomb) might escape observation. Clandestine tests of this type could not create any significant security risks however, since higher yield weapons are already available for response and deterrence against the first use of neutron weapons.

In view of the large number of tests the United States and the U.S.S.R. have already conducted, it would seem that the gains from halting the race between nuclear-weapon states for more sophisticated designs and from erecting barriers to the proliferation of nuclear weapons to additional states would more than offset the risks of a secret violation of a comprehensive ban by very low yield testing.

PEACEFUL NUCLEAR EXPLOSIONS

The second key issue which must be resolved to achieve a comprehensive test ban is how to deal with peaceful nuclear explosions, i.e., those carried out to provide some non-military economic benefit.

The concept of using nuclear explosives for peaceful purposes was first investigated by the United States in the late 1950s. The Soviet Union was not initially enthusiastic about the concept. When the Limited Test Ban Treaty was negotiated, the Soviet Union refused to allow the inclusion of any exception to permit peaceful nuclear tests. Soviet negotiators suggested that this could be dealt with later, if and when peaceful nuclear explosions became practical, a precedent which could be followed for a comprehensive ban. Because of this Soviet objection, the Limited Test Ban Treaty did ban all peaceful nuclear tests in which radioactive debris would be vented into the atmosphere and carried beyond the borders of the country conducting the test. There have been several instances of technical violations of this ban, as for example in 1965 when a Soviet explosion to dam a river sent radioactive debris out over Japan and other countries, where it was detected and measured.

In recent years U.S. studies have shown less and less potential value for peaceful nuclear explosions. The American program is now virtually at a standstill. On the other hand, the Soviet Union became more and more interested in peaceful

13

nuclear explosions. On at least one occasion it extinguished an underground gas fire with a peaceful nuclear explosion.[2] The current major Soviet interest is the possible excavation of the Pechora-Kama Canal which would divert waters flowing into the Arctic Ocean south into the Caspian Basin. This was the Soviet justification for insisting on a threshold as high as 150 kilotons for the recent threshold and peaceful nuclear explosion treaties. Such a project would require hundreds of high-yield explosives and would inevitably send large quantities of radioactive debris outside the borders of the Soviet Union. Therefore, to dig such a canal with peaceful nuclear explosions, the U.S.S.R. would either have to have the Limited Test Ban Treaty amended or else be in flagrant violation. World sentiment would be strongly opposed to such a downgrading of the Limited Test Ban Treaty.

Other possible uses, involving contained explosions which are not contrary to the Limited Test Ban Treaty, include the freeing of oil from shale, releasing natural gas from certain hard geologic formations, and *in situ* leaching of copper. None appears economically attractive at the moment, and all would require large numbers of sophisticated nuclear explosives. The appeal of peaceful nuclear explosions is apparently waning, but several nations are not yet prepared to forego the option.

Unfortunately a nuclear explosive designed to serve some peaceful purpose cannot be readily distinguished from one designed to kill people in war. In fact peaceful explosions often require some of the same, highly sophisticated design features as nuclear weapons in order to be safe and economical for civil use. This fact of life was recognized when the Non-Proliferation Treaty was negotiated. Under that agreement, only nuclear-weapon states were allowed to develop peaceful nuclear explosions, the benefits of which these states were then pledged to make available to non-nuclear nations on a cost basis. This same indistinguishability problem, in a more difficult form, must be resolved in a comprehensive test ban treaty in order to prevent any nation, nuclear or non-nuclear, from circumventing the ban on weapons tests under the guise of a peaceful explosion.

Since no verification procedures, even the most intrusive on-site inspections, hold much promise for preventing a peaceful nuclear explosion test from being used as a cover for military experiments, peaceful nuclear explosions, if continued, would appear to present an almost insurmountable barrier to a ban on weapons tests. Certainly the verification loophole is much larger than any provided by the shortcomings in seismic capabilities, which have held up a comprehensive test ban treaty for so long. However, the potential benefits of peaceful nuclear explosions appear marginal at best and certainly of no importance in the near future. Excavation or vented explosions have already been banned by the Limited Test Ban Treaty, and contained explosions require much more detailed study to determine whether they can be made safe and economical and whether they provide real advantages over more conventional methods of performing the same mission. Since most engineering applications of nuclear devices will require large numbers, hundreds or thousands, of sophisticated explosives, their conduct will become practical only for nations with large nuclear programs.

Thus there seems to be no basis for sacrificing the opportunity to stop all weapons testing in order to maintain the option (over the next few years) to partake of the undemonstrated benefits of peaceful nuclear explosions. This problem might be handled under a comprehensive test ban by declaring a moratorium on all peaceful tests for a five-year period during which the International Atomic Energy Agency (IAEA), other groups and individual nations could study further the potential uses, possible verification procedures, and international management of their conduct, if and when they are deemed economically beneficial. The moratorium must be long enough to ensure that it halts weapons development rather than simply postpones weapons testing until the end of the period.* After five years, an international conference could decide whether the moratorium should be continued or whether some new method for dealing with the problem ought to be developed.

WHO MUST SIGN A COMPREHENSIVE TEST BAN TREATY?

A long-term position of the Soviet Union has been that all nuclear-weapon states must be parties to a comprehensive test ban treaty for it to come into force. The United States, on the other hand, while seeking maximum participation, has held that only the participation of the United States and the U.S.S.R. is necessary for it to be effective. Because China and perhaps France are unlikely to sign a comprehensive test ban treaty initially, the Soviet position, if not modified, is tantamount to deferring indefinitely the achievement of a ban on all nuclear tests. Since most nations of the world strongly desire that nu-

---

*On November 2, 1977, General Secretary Brezhnev dropped earlier Soviet insistence that suspension of nuclear explosions permit relatively low-yield blasts for peaceful purposes, saying, "We are prepared to reach agreement on a moratorium covering nuclear explosions for peaceful purposes along with a ban on all nuclear weapons tests for a definite period."

clear testing be halted or at least drastically reduced at an early date and since a treaty might be even more difficult to negotiate if additional countries acquire nuclear weapons, some way must be found to resolve the parties problem.

The U.S.S.R. already agreed to the principle of limited participation when it signed the Threshold Test Ban Treaty, which applies only to the United States and the U.S.S.R. It, therefore, should not be inalterably opposed, at least temporarily, to limited participation. In the next five to ten years neither China nor France could develop any new types of weapons that would stimulate renewed testing by the U.S.S.R. or the United States to redress imbalances. Therefore, the issue could possibly be resolved in a comprehensive ban with an article stating that the treaty's continuation would be reviewed after five years if all nuclear-weapon states had not become parties by then. Further, all such arms control treaties contain a standard escape clause, which allows a nation to withdraw from its obligations if extraordinary events related to the subject matter of the treaty have jeopardized the supreme interests of that nation. Such provisions should be more than satisfactory to deal with any emergencies which might arise because all nuclear-weapon states were not parties. Therefore, this should not continue to be a major roadblock to a comprehensive test ban treaty. It is surely better to stop U.S. and Soviet testing than to allow them to continue just because all others will not join in.

UNWILLINGNESS TO STOP TESTING

A normally unspoken, but probably fundamental reason that a comprehensive test ban has not been achieved to date is that the existing nuclear-weapon states, or at least strong elements within them, wish to continue testing in order to refine still further their nuclear stockpiles and keep their weapons laboratories active.

Weapons designers can always find ways of improving already available weapons, but after more than 1,000 tests over thirty years, both the United States and the U.S.S.R. have acquired such sophisticated arsenals that further testing can only provide very marginal gains. Even if no further testing were allowed, they would still have some device or design available which would be suitable, if not optimal, for any new delivery system. It is hard to see how either nation's security could be impaired by an inability to test, and the gains from stopping all tests should more than outweigh any possible disadvantages.

There is also a demand for reliability tests of existing weapons to make sure they continue to operate properly after years in storage. However, such proof-testing, though permitted currently, has rarely if ever been practiced, so giving up the option to do so would not constitute a major sacrifice.

Nevertheless, the habits of weapons developers and those who set requirements do not change easily. Therefore, it will continue to be important to marshal every argument to convince governments that the risks of continued testing are real and the gains from a comprehensive test ban treaty overriding.

Program For the U.N. Special Session on Disarmament

A key element in providing a stable regime under a comprehensive test ban will be an international mechanism for resolving the inevitable ambiguities that will occur. Even with the best verification capabilities there will always be events which could lead to suspicions that one or another nation was violating the provisions of the treaty and seeking some political or military advantage. The Special Session could profitably explore multilateral versions of the bilateral Standing Consultative Commission such as a multinational consultative commission. Such an organization could review data and information provided by "national technical means of verification" (nonintrusive inspection devices, such as photographic satellites) and provide a forum for clearing up any misunderstandings. It could provide the means for arranging visits to specific locations within any nation in which there was an unexplained event to give reassurance that a clandestine test had not occurred. It might also provide an international data center. The U.N. Special Session provides a unique opportunity to plan in advance for such a multinational commission, which could be formally established when a comprehensive test ban had been signed.

Since peaceful nuclear explosions are a serious roadblock to a treaty and since there is widespread international confusion over their potential, another goal for the Special Session could be to review existing studies on peaceful nuclear explosions, such as that by the International Atomic Energy Agency, and, where necessary, commission continuing research and review programs in order to have a more definitive picture of their feasibility five years hence. The Special Session should urge that a comprehensive test ban treaty include provisions for a peaceful nuclear test moratorium to be reviewed at the end of five years.

The Special Session will provide an excellent forum to mobilize international public opinion in support of an immediate halt to all nuclear testing. Those states continuing to test must be made to realize the importance that other countries around the world attach to this issue. The comprehensive test ban treaty should be made the symbol of whether the world is prepared to downgrade the political and military significance of nuclear weapons. Pressures should be exerted on all nations to become parties to a comprehensive test ban treaty, and the international political penalties of intransigence on making a commitment to forego testing should be emphasized.

Notes

1. For a report of the key policy statement by Prime Minister Morarji Desai on July 13, 1977, see Mohan Ram, "India Bows to Carter, Ruling Out More A-tests" *Christian Science Monitor,* July 20, 1977.

2. For details of Soviet use of peaceful nuclear explosions, see Milo D. Nordyke, "A Review of Soviet Data on the Peaceful Uses of Nuclear Explosions," *Annals of Nuclear Energy Vol. II* (Oxford: Penguin Press, 1975).

Steps to Halt Nuclear Proliferation

Francesco Calogero

Nuclear weapons have been employed in war only twice: on August 6, 1945, over Hiroshima and three days later, over Nagasaki. The single explosion of the Hiroshima bomb, which had an estimated yield of thirteen kilotons, killed over 80 thousand persons and injured at least as many.[1]

In 1945 only the United States possessed nuclear weapons. Now the arsenals of the five nuclear-weapon countries contain many thousands of operational weapons, and many of these are hundreds, or even thousands, of times more powerful than the Hiroshima bomb. Yet nuclear weapons have not been used in war since the Nagasaki explosion thirty-two years ago. Certainly a major reason for this restraint is that only a few countries have acquired a nuclear weapons capability up to now.

Over the *next* three decades however, unless steps are taken to strengthen the current non-proliferation regime, many more states, and perhaps even some non-governmental groups, are likely to acquire nuclear weapons. The technological barriers that have impeded widespread proliferation until now are becoming more and more permeable, due to the increased availability of fissile materials and nuclear know-how which are the inevitable by-products of expanding nuclear energy facilities. Few people believe that with more nuclear-weapon states the same sort of restraint that has prevented the "use-in-anger" of nuclear weapons over the past thirty-two years can continue. Indeed, the spread of nuclear weapons would increase the risk not only of their use by new international actors, but would also

19

provide the most likely mechanism whereby the present nuclear-weapon states, especially the two superpowers, might be drawn into a nuclear conflict, with the cataclysmic consequences implied by the enormous and continuing increase in the lethality of their nuclear arsenals. Therefore most people agree that every effort should be made to impede the spread of nuclear weapons, either to additional countries or to non-governmental groups, and the U.N. Special Session provides a timely opportunity to focus on the steps which must be taken to avert further proliferation.

Steps to Halt Governmental Proliferation

Eliminate international conflicts. The root motivations for the acquisition and eventual use of weapons originate from existing and potential conflicts; if all these could be eliminated, there would be no need to worry about nuclear proliferation (nor about much else). The fact that this is obvious does not imply it is altogether negligible. Moreover, at the root of most conflicts are the inequities of our present world, where too many people are still deprived of bare essentials: food, shelter, medical care and basic education. No recipe for the easy elimination of these inequities is at hand, yet it is unwise to ignore them in a world characterized by a growing awareness of these inequities and by the likely spread of tremendous destructive potentialities such as those associated with nuclear weapons.

De-emphasize the role of nuclear weapons. Clearly the urge to "go nuclear" is proportional to the relevance that the possession of nuclear weapons has in international affairs. Nuclear weapons play a fundamental role in the strategic posture of the nuclear-weapon countries, and in particular of the superpowers; it would not be possible, nor advisable, to belittle their importance in order to induce others not to strive for their possession. But it is also implicit in their nature as "ultimate" instruments that nuclear weapons are largely useless as political or military tools. Possession of an enormous nuclear arsenal aid not prevent the United States from losing the Vietnam war. Similarly, the United Kingdom or France, with all their "nukes," were essentially in the same position as the Federal Republic of Germany or Italy when confronted by the oil embargo. Indeed, it is recognition of this "uselessness" that constitutes the basic disincentive for many countries to acquire nuclear weapons.

It is thus this quality of uselessness that ought to be emphasized to support a non-proliferation policy; all developments that go in the opposite direction—making nuclear weapons

20

more "usable" and emphasizing their political relevance—are instead effective inducements to proliferation. Specific examples are the development of relatively "discriminate" nuclear weapons like the so-called "mini-nukes" and the "neutron bomb." More generally, any move that tends to blur the operational distinction between nuclear and conventional weapons should be avoided. Indeed, it should be emphasized that even discussion of these developments (especially in the "salesman" fashion generally adopted by the representatives of the weapons labs who try to sell these concepts within the American decision-making system) is a sharp stimulant to proliferation. Such arguments provide powerful ammunition to advocates of the acquisition of an independent nuclear option who exist, in more or less disguised form, in most countries. Indeed, there is such a coincidence of arguments and interests as to justify the suspicion of an effective link between certain groups in the nuclear-weapon countries having a vested interest in an expanded military and political role for nuclear weapons and those in non-nuclear-weapon countries who advocate the acquisition of an independent nuclear option.

Another stimulant to proliferation is the notion that nuclear weapons have political relevance. While largely contradicted by facts, this concept is generally emphasized by those who, within the decision-making system of the nuclear-weapon countries, argue for an expanded program of nuclear armaments. A rather extreme version of this notion was apparent in former U.S. Defense Secretary James Schlesinger's attempt to give political significance to any perceived imbalance of strategic nuclear power, even if admittedly devoid of military relevance.[2]

These stimuli to proliferation provide the political background that fuels and favors the pressure groups which in most countries, more or less openly, advocate the nuclear weapons option. Indeed, the atmosphere they create is a fertile breeding ground for the security and prestige arguments, tied to the specific situation of each country, which are used to advocate the acquisition of an autonomous nuclear option. These influences are cumulative and pervasive, but because it is difficult to pin down specific cause and effect, they tend to be underestimated. The examples mentioned above (mini-nukes, neutron bomb, Schlesinger's statement) are representative, but clearly what counts most is the general approach to strategic matters and especially the role attributed to nuclear weapons.

The stimuli to proliferation cited here are all taken from the United States; this is not to imply that other examples could not be given from other nuclear powers, only that—because of their remarkably open system of government—American ex-

21

perience tends to establish the tone of strategic thinking world-wide.

Halt vertical proliferation. The best that any anti-proliferation policy can achieve is to delay the spread of nuclear weapons, but this development is bound to occur eventually unless the present nuclear-weapon states give some clear indication of moving away from reliance on nuclear weapons both for their own security and for that of the international system as a whole. Short of unilateral restraints, such an indication can probably best come from a breakthrough at the Strategic Arms Limitation Talks (SALT), signaling the beginning of a process to rein in, and then reverse, the strategic arms race.

The strategic balance between the United States and the Soviet Union is relatively stable, and the danger of proliferation is a much more serious threat to their security than any marginal imbalances in some strategic unit of account. Both superpowers therefore have much to gain from quick and significant progress at SALT (almost irrespective of the details of the agreement). Both stand to lose much from a stalemate, or, even worse, from a failure to agree which might result in further escalation that would inevitably encourage proliferation.

This general argument seems compelling even if it points to a cause-effect mechanism that cannot be displayed in fine detail. Who can doubt that nuclear proliferation will occur, to a significant extent and in a short time (say, within our lifetimes), unless a considerable change occurs in the international role of nuclear weapons?

The superpowers have committed themselves through the Non-Proliferation Treaty to curb vertical proliferation "at an early date." If this commitment is not honored, then the non-nuclear-weapon countries will find it increasingly difficult to keep their part of the deal—much as it may be against their own best interest to go nuclear. Indeed, is it not against the superpowers' own best interest to continue their vertical arms race?

Finally, it would be hard to conceive of a more effective stimulant for proliferation than the advent of the long-range cruise missile. This opens the prospect for many non-nuclear-weapon countries, should they ever decide to go militarily nuclear, of acquiring a force that makes some strategic sense and the cost of which—in economic and technological terms—does not appear beyond reach. Indeed, this development opens the long-term prospect for many countries to acquire a credible threat even against the superpowers themselves. This possibility is certainly not around the corner, but from a political and psychological point of view it makes a significant difference. What before the advent of the long-range cruise missile appeared unobtainable may now seem within conceivable reach. This kind of consideration is going to influence military thinking. and eventually planning, in many countries, and the effects will show up in the next one or two decades.

It appears, therefore, unwise on the part of the United States to spur this development. Unfortunately, because the cruise missile is so technologically attractive and so difficult to identify in view of its ubiquitous role, its advent has been to some extent inevitable, like that of a natural calamity. Moreover, the decision to proceed with its development has not been subject to critical evaluation, due to its entanglement with the SALT negotiations and because it was used by the Carter administration as a *quid pro quo* for the internal political acceptance of the termination of the B-1 bomber program. The fact remains that this is a disastrous trend, from the point of view of proliferation as well as for its general impact on arms control prospects.

Restraint on development of the cruise missile would have served the best interest of the United States and of the rest of the world. Whether the cat is out of the bag for good, or whether there is still some possibility to limit the damage, is something that remains to be seen. This will depend not only on developments at SALT in the immediate future, but also on unilateral decisions on the extent and detailed nature of the cruise missiles that will be developed and deployed.

Indeed, if the logic advocated here were to prevail—namely, if the proliferatory implications of strategic decisions were given top priority, in recognition of the primacy of the danger of nuclear proliferation—there would be much less reluctance on the part of the superpowers to undertake unilateral initiatives in the direction of restraint. There is ample scope for such initiatives, directed towards de-emphasizing the relevance of nuclear weapons and curbing the vertical arms race, without undermining the immediate or long-range security of the superpowers. If the examples discussed above refer mainly to the United States, clearly the same arguments apply equally to the Soviet Union.

Ban all nuclear testing. The single measure that would contribute most significantly to non-proliferation and which could be agreed upon immediately, would be the conclusion of a comprehensive ban on all nuclear testing. This issue is treated elsewhere in this volume and will not be enlarged upon here.

Support and strengthen the Non-Proliferation Treaty. Despite its shortcomings—lack of universal acceptance and unsatisfactory performance of the nuclear-weapon parties to fulfill their commitments under Article VI—the Non-Proliferation Treaty remains the fundamental instrument of any anti-proliferation strategy. For many countries that have acceded to it, the treaty provides an effective barrier against the temptation to go nuclear, by making it impossible to take such a decision without a large debate involving essentially the whole decision-making system. It should be noted that up to now, the decision to undertake a program aimed at acquiring a nuclear explosives capability has always been made in secret by small groups within national governments. With the existence of the Non-Proliferation Treaty it becomes much more difficult for the advocates of a nuclear option to make their case inside the bureaucracy, and the more dangerous promoters of proliferation are rendered ineffective.

In the countries that have not acceded to the Non-Proliferation Treaty, the existence of an international regime that has gained large, if not universal, acceptance is the best argument that can be used by the internal groups who oppose the decision to go nuclear. The verification clauses of the treaty provide a reasonably reliable guarantee that the countries that have acceded to it do not have in progress a secret program aimed at the development of nuclear weapons. This is important, because it prevents the onset of rumors that might be manipulated to stampede public opinion and/or the ruling elites to listen with a more sympathetic ear to the advocacy of the acquisition of a nuclear option.

Clearly the Non-Proliferation Treaty is not, by itself, sufficient to impede proliferation indefinitely. But it would be a great mistake to weaken support for it now. While other international initiatives to complement the Non-Proliferation Treaty are welcome and may be useful, this does not imply that it has failed or is in any sense unworthy of support. On the contrary, all Non-Proliferation Treaty commitments should be honored, and a policy which favors treaty partners and tries to extend the non-proliferation regime to non-partners (for instance as regards safeguards) should be pursued. The same positive attitude should be taken towards other initiatives that are congruent with the spirit of the Non-Proliferation Treaty.

Ensure adequate non-proliferatory supplies of nuclear energy. Clearly it would be disastrous if the competition between nuclear suppliers were to develop into a race to provide technologies having a weapons potential (typically plutonium reprocessing and uranium separation). The sales by France to Pakistan and by West Germany to Brazil, to the extent they appear steps in this direction, constitute a dangerous precedent; one can only hope that they do not actually result in the delivery of reprocessing and separation capabilities to separation capabilities to countries that would be likely to divert them to weapon purposes.

The worldwide development of nuclear energy has important economic implications, and the suspicion that an alleged anti-proliferation policy serves merely to promote national interests is hard to dispel. For instance, while non-proliferation appears to be the dominant motivation behind the Carter administration decision to delay as long as possible any commitment to a nuclear energy economy based on plutonium re-cycling, there are those in the European nuclear industry who suspect that industrial competition between the United States and Western Europe (where some claim breeder technology is more advanced) could be an important factor in the new American policy.

Because such economic interests do exist and motivations are always mixed, it is doubtful whether either side can convince the other of its good intentions. Recognition by all of the universal danger implicit in proliferation is urgently required, and elimination of this danger should take priority over economic evaluations. This line of thought cannot prevail, however, unless the issue is taken to the top level of decision-making. To be explicit, decisions affecting the French deal with Pakistan or the German deal with Brazil may, and probably will, be affected only by negotiations directly between heads of state. Consultation mechanisms between suppliers at a much lower level may not be very useful. Furthermore, while meetings of experts can serve to map out technical details, there is a danger that nuclear energy technocrats will tend to downgrade the risks of proliferation, given their vested interest in expanding the nuclear industry.

Because issues of economic competition refer mainly to the Western camp and because the United States must lead a non-proliferation policy for it to have any chance of success, the issue boils down essentially to the question of whether the U.S. government is willing and able to rally the main nuclear suppliers around a policy that gives high priority to non-proliferation. This can be done only if the U.S. administration is prepared to do two things: exert pressures at the highest level for the acceptance of such a policy and offer a fair economic deal to the other partners, for instance, by letting them have a part of the world market, even if this involves a certain economic sacrifice on the part of the American nuclear industry.

Given this background, it seems clear to me that the main question is neither the institutional form of the "suppliers' club" nor its expansion by the inclusion of marginal countries in the hopes of appeasing them. On the contrary a certain amount of ruthlessness is probably needed, and this is probably better implemented by a more restricted group. The possibility that such a policy might produce adverse effects, in the sense of forcing countries to go in directions that have a proliferatory potential (e.g. build reprocessing facilities of their own), does not depend on the type of forum in which such a policy is developed but rather on its substance. The essential goal is to offer a supply of nuclear fuel at fair prices and to guarantee this with certainty (this may require shared, or international, owning of multinational facilities) so that there will be no economic, or political, justification for developing national reprocessing and separation facilities, other than the clear intent to acquire a weapons option.[3] If this goal is not realized speedily, reprocessing and perhaps also separation facilities will inevitably mushroom.

Of course technological developments, such as isotopic laser separation, may eventually open new possibilities to secure materials for nuclear weapons which will be rather difficult to control. But even if these developments materialize, there is considerable difference between the decision to build special facilities for a military-oriented program and the decision to divert nuclear materials (be it highly enriched uranium or plutonium) to weapons from existing facilities originally built for peaceful purposes. Indeed the very possession of such materials might be viewed as a permanent temptation. Thus, a policy aimed at preventing the emergence of national reprocessing and separation plants, especially in countries not party to the Non-Proliferation Treaty, will always remain important.

Another, and possibly more important, role of a suppliers club is in connection with the physical security of nuclear materials (see below).

Pursuit of a technological fix. The hope of inventing a method of producing nuclear energy which does not at the same time facilitate an eventual nuclear weapons program does not appear justified at present.

However, a detailed evaluation of all elements of the nuclear energy cycle from the point of view of their susceptibility to diversion to weapons purposes would be useful. Research programs to explore alternative routes which maximize the technological difficulties of diversion (even at some economic cost) should be vigorously pursued. Nevertheless, politicians and diplomats must realize that the potential to halt proliferation by technological fix is inherently limited.

Clarify the peaceful nuclear explosions issue. Many millions of dollars have been wasted in the United States searching for peaceful applications of nuclear explosions. A powerful lobby, closely associated with the weapons laboratories, was behind this activity and occasionally used it to create impediments to arms control negotiations (for instance, on the test ban). Eventually the American decision-making system has come to recognize the uselessness of the peaceful nuclear explosion concept. Ironically, it was in the Soviet Union where the technologists in favor of peaceful nuclear explosions acquired later influence (possibly as a belated effect of the American program) and convinced their leadership that this option could not be given up. While the Soviet rationale may be somewhat more justifiable than the American for reasons of geography, a large measure of skepticism remains appropriate. In any case, late in 1977, the Soviet leadership announced its willingness to forego peaceful nuclear explosions in order to achieve a comprehensive nuclear test ban.

There can be little doubt, however, that a peaceful nuclear explosion program constitutes for a non-nuclear-weapon country the most convenient route from a political point of view—both internationally and internally—to justify the undertaking of a project aimed at acquiring a nuclear explosive capability. The Indian example is a case in point.

An anti-proliferatory policy should first of all take a hard look at claims for the economic advantages of peaceful nuclear explosions, having a clear understanding of the proliferatory stimulus they imply. It should, moreover, proceed to implement quietly the provisions of Article V of the Non-Proliferation Treaty, taking due care not to promulgate the notion that peaceful nuclear explosions are useful.[4] If the need to utilize these peaceful explosions is put forward by some national group trying to pressure for the acquisition of an autonomous capability to produce nuclear explosives, the objection should then be *readily* available that, if ever peaceful nuclear explosions were needed, they could be more conveniently performed in the framework of the regime outlined in Article V of the Non-Proliferation Treaty. And the peaceful nuclear explosions issue should not be allowed to impede the achievement of a comprehensive test ban.

Promote non-nuclear energy alternatives. An international program directed to the promotion of energy conservation and of non-nuclear energy sources (solar, geothermal, wind, tidal, etc.) should be launched immediately. It should be led and financed by the technologically advanced United States, the Soviet Union, Europe, Japan, and so on. It should be largely aimed at offering energy alternatives that are more convenient

27

and appropriate than nuclear energy, especially for small and developing countries.

Such an "energy for development" program should be on a large scale and ideally would combine research, technological development, and industrial assistance, on multinational or bilateral bases. As a new international organization it could serve to counterbalance the promotion of nuclear energy implied by the activities of the International Atomic Energy Agency and begin to redress economic and technological distortions brought about by the large hidden subsidy that nuclear energy has obtained relative to other energy sources, due to its military applications. Contribution to the running costs of such an effort by the major powers should be amply justified by its long-range security implications in terms of the reduced likelihood of nuclear proliferation, but it would also yield economic and technological benefits to the advanced countries themselves as well as its primary aim of aiding the less developed. The indispensability of nuclear power for meeting the world's energy requirements need not be questioned in order to support the search for alternative energy sources.

Steps to Halt Non-Governmental Proliferation

Guarantee the physical security of fissile material. Some consider the prospects of non-governmental nuclear weapons proliferation quite likely, while others emphasize the technological difficulties standing in the way of such projects.[5] There is, however, universal agreement on the need to guarantee the physical security of fissile materials. This is an international problem insofar as material stolen in one country could be used for terrorism or blackmail in another—be the motive political or economic. At present the threat to explode a nuclear device or a radiological bomb made of plutonium would be hardly credible. (Although as examples have shown, it would be taken very seriously; however low its credibility, the risk is immense.) How much worse would be the situation after a theft involving, say, 20 kilograms of plutonium!

It is sometimes pointed out that there are other, simpler, forms of terrorism or blackmail that could be attempted, involving for instance biological agents rather than nuclear materials. This hardly seems a valid argument for not worrying about the security of nuclear materials and facilities. (Indeed, what is simple for one person may be more difficult for another; an extremist who has a job in a nuclear establishment and opts for terrorism will naturally be attracted by the opportunity to seize or steal nuclear materials, especially if they are inadequately protected.) There is, moreover, a purely economic incentive for stealing fissile materials, and such thefts may be relevant to government proliferation, if the rumored existence of a black market for fissile materials has any foundation. (Standing offers to buy fissile materials at astronomical prices are attributed to various governments.)

Fissile materials and nuclear facilities are not well protected at present and there is little hope the situation will improve drastically, at least until the first major instance of robbery or sabotage is known to have occurred. Action on this issue should be undertaken immediately, either by the International Atomic Energy Agency or the London Suppliers Group, but in any event with the firm commitment of both the United States and the Soviet Union.

The Carter administration has been notable for its clear statement of the high priority assigned to the prevention of nuclear-weapon proliferation. It is to be hoped similar priority will be accorded to the need to consider the physical security of fissile materials worldwide as a matter directly relevant to U.S. and international security. This should imply the readiness to devote to this problem a small fraction of the resources that are spent for defense.

Clearly the United States cannot, and should not, protect nuclear materials and facilities in other countries. But it might create a body of advisors ready to provide guidance and, if need be, equipment to the countries that are willing to accept it. The United States should also support the establishment of a similar body on an international basis in the framework of or in association with the institutions mentioned above. A crucial question in this respect is the cost. While it is clear that eventually every country should bear the cost of protecting its own nuclear plants, it is also clear that to set up speedily the required system of physical safeguards, the United States, preferably joined by other countries that devote vast resources to defense expenses and have a strong interest in preventing international terrorism, should be prepared to offer and provide assistance disregarding the cost this may entail—namely using the same sort of attitude that prevails when the provision of military assistance is deemed necessary for security considerations. If such an initiative were instrumental in preventing only one major theft of nuclear materials over the next few years it would be highly cost-effective, in terms of its impact on the security of the United States and of many other industrialized countries, and its cost need not exceed a small fraction of their defense outlays.

There is one implicit danger in this proposal, namely, that it might result in yet another hidden subsidy to nuclear energy, not to mention a possible outcry against foreign meddling in internal affairs. But the risk of doing nothing or of relying on national initiatives is too serious, especially if one envisions the extreme scenario (perhaps unlikely, but not impossible after a major nuclear theft) of the threat of a nuclear explosion in a city. An accusation of foreign meddling in internal affairs would hardly be justified if collaboration were offered rather than imposed, especially if it were possible to organize it in an international framework. It might then be reasonably expected that many governments would, in some form or other, take advantage of it.

Joint leadership focusing on measures to guarantee the physical security of fissile materials and nuclear facilities by the United States and the Soviet Union would probably catalyze much broader international support. It may also produce some adverse reactions, for instance, from liberal intellectuals worrying about the prospect of close and effective CIA-KGB cooperation aimed at preventing actions that might originate from political groups with well-justified grievances. But what is the alternative? Can human society accept the prospect of the use of nuclear weapons by terrorists?

The specific measures that could be taken to eliminate, or at least decrease, the risk of nuclear theft or sabotage have been extensively analyzed in recent years and will not be dealt with in any detail here, except to note that co-location of nuclear facilities is a measure generally recommended in connection with the suppliers' club.[6] Thus, consideration of physical security may reinforce the notion of large nuclear centers that could be multinationally or internationally owned and/or controlled, which would provide extensive services (including separation and, if need be, reprocessing) to many national customers.

It should be emphasized that the most direct route for nongovernmental proliferation at present would be seizure of ready-made nuclear weapons, thousands of which are deployed in vulnerable sites around the world. Safeguarding these weapons against terrorism is an urgent task in everyone's best interest.

Conclusion

Several years ago a serious international effort to cope with the problem of nuclear proliferation was undertaken by the international community. Its outcome was the opening of the Non-Proliferation Treaty for signature on July 1, 1968. Thereafter the major powers have constantly paid lip service to the need to prevent proliferation but have in fact given very low priority to this issue.

The current American administration, led by a former nuclear engineer, has focused on the danger of nuclear proliferation as a central issue of international security. President Carter's message to Congress in April, 1977, submitting the administration's Nuclear Non-Proliferation Act of 1977, begins with the statement: "The need to halt nuclear proliferation is one of mankind's most pressing challenges." The bill itself contains many detailed provisions aimed at preventing the export of nuclear materials and technologies that might have a proliferatory impact. It also recognizes the need to act on motivations, especially with respect to the availability of an assured fuel supply.[7]

Portions of this bill have already been emasculated by the Congress, but there have also been some positive results. The plant at Barnwell, South Carolina, for example, has been denied a license for the domestic reprocessing of spent fuel, and the commercialization of the fast breeder has been slowed down, though in the autumn of 1977 the fate of the Clinch River facility still hung in the balance. In addition, there have been some responses from other nuclear supplier countries in the form of verbal assurances of more prudent nuclear export policies and restraints on reprocessing.

Yet a view of the proliferation issue limited to questions of nuclear export is certainly inadequate. The problems of nuclear proliferation cannot be separated from the general attitude towards nuclear weapons, including the attitudes of the existing nuclear-weapon states.

This paper has largely ignored a basic issue relevant to proliferation, namely the security needs and perceptions of specific countries. Indeed, these can be discussed only on a case-by-case basis. But a non-proliferation policy must also have a comprehensive aspect, and its requirements are directly relevant to the overall strategic policy of all major powers, especially of the two superpowers. Arguments to support this view have been detailed above, as well as the specific indications of the elements of strategic policy that are more relevant to proliferation.

This paper ends with a summary of recommended steps toward achievement of a non-proliferation regime, which are offered as guidelines to delegates to the U.N. Special Session on Disarmament. What must be stressed in conclusion, however, is the primary need for an agreement between the two superpowers to put the nuclear arms race under control and to achieve that degree of bilateral collaboration and cooperation which will enable them to lead an effective international movement towards non-proliferation objectives—and to do so in time to avoid global disaster.

Summary: Non-Proliferation and the Special Session

The delegates to the Special Session should focus on how best to achieve the following steps.

- Recognition of the dangers implicit in nuclear proliferation, and the assigning of top priority to its prevention by the international community.

- An end to the nuclear arms competition between the United States and the U.S.S.R. as an indispensable condition for avoiding further proliferation. This implies the de-emphasis of nuclear weapons as viable instruments of national security policies.

- A comprehensive ban on all nuclear explosions.

- Implementation of further nuclear-free zones.

- Strengthening of the Non-Proliferation Treaty by giving preferential treatment to parties in terms of providing nuclear technology under effective safeguards, and by implementing Article V.

- Establishment of an international regime to reduce incentives to acquire and sell nuclear technologies with a proliferative potential. Assured long-term fuel supplies should be guaranteed at equitable prices and cut-throat competition between nuclear suppliers must be avoided.

- Promotion of non-nuclear energy sources, preferably through an international agency.

- Guarantee the physical security of both fissile material and existing nuclear materials against theft and sabotage.

Notes

1. See Frank Barnaby and Joseph Rotblat "Hiroshima and Nagasaki: the Survivors" in *New Scientist* (UK), August 25, 1977.

2. "There is also an important relationship between the political behavior of many leaders of other nations and what they perceive the strategic nuclear balance to be. By no means do all of them engage in the dynamic calculations about the interactions of Soviet and U.S. forces that have so affected our judgments in the past. However, many do react to the static measures of relative force size, number of warheads, equivalent megatonnage, and so forth. Hence, to the degree that we wish to influence the perceptions of others, we

must take appropriate steps (by their lights) in the design of the strategic forces." Secretary of Defense J.R. Schlesinger, *Annual Defense Department Report, FY 1975*, March 4, 1974, p. 27.

3. See, for instance, Lincoln P. Bloomfield, "Nuclear Spread and World Order" *Foreign Affairs*, Vol. 53 No. 1 (July 1975), pp. 743-755.

4. See Appendix II for the text of the Non-Proliferation Treaty.

5. See, for instance, John McPhee, *The Curve of Binding Energy* (New York: Farrar, Straus & Giroux, 1973) and Mason Willrich and Theodore B. Taylor, *Nuclear Theft: Risks and Safeguards* (Cambridge, Mass.: Ballinger, 1974).

6. See Wilrich and Taylor, *op. cit.* and "Nuclear Terrorism" in Spurgeon M. Keeney, Jr., ed., *Nuclear Power: Issues and Choices* (Cambridge, Mass.: Ballinger, 1977.)

7. See Appendix III for the text of President Carter's message to the Congress.

Nuclear-Weapon-Free Zones

An Effective Instrument for Disarmament

Alfonso García Robles

The establishment of nuclear-weapon-free zones constitutes one of the most effective means for non-nuclear states to prevent the proliferation of nuclear weapons and achieve disarmament.[1] For this reason, it is unfortunate that various nations raised so many objections and created such opposition to the creation of these zones in the 1950s and early 1960s when the question first arose in the United Nations. Since 1956, the United Nations General Assembly has repeatedly discussed the eventual creation of nuclear-weapon-free zones in various regions, among them Central Europe, Africa, the Middle East, the Balkans, the Mediterranean, Scandinavia, Asia and the Pacific, and, finally, Latin America.[2] Nonetheless, Central Europe, Africa and Latin America have been the only regions where formal, concrete proposals have been submitted and seriously considered.

In the course of the debates over nuclear-weapon-free zones, various participants, after recognizing that the creation of the zones is primarily the concern of those states within the zone, began to impose a growing number of conditions, some of them impossible to meet, which, in their opinion, would be indispensable to the establishment of such zones. To the extent such conditions would have nullified the rights of zone states to determine the nature of the zone, they contradict the notion that self-determination is the critical element in the establishment of these zones. In addition such conditions would seem to ignore that the United Nations has set forth in the first chapter of its charter the principle of sovereign equality of all its members. For a militarily denuclearized zone to have full juridical validity it would suffice that governments make the decision to sign the appropriate treaties or accords in the free exercise of their sovereignty.[3]

The Treaty for the Prohibition of Nuclear Weapons in Latin America (Treaty of Tlatelolco) has expressly eliminated the requirement that all zone states originally participate in the creation of a nuclear-weapon-free zone.[4] The treaty has decisively strengthened the position of those who have long rejected such a requirement and has virtually eliminated any articulation of the opposing view. Although support of such a requirement is still discernible in the interventions of some "government experts" involved in a "comprehensive study of the question of nuclear-weapon-free zones in all its aspects" solicited by the United Nations General Assembly in its twenty-ninth session,[5] it is clear that such a view reflects anachronistic considerations now abandoned by the vast majority of states.[6] This should readily be seen by the adoption of resolution 3472 B (XXX) by the General Assembly on December 11, 1975, which includes two basic definitions on the subject, the first on "the concept of a nuclear-weapon-free zone" and the second on "the principal obligations of the nuclear-weapon States towards nuclear-weapon-free zones and towards the States included therein."[7]

The following considerations, expressed in the Conference of the Committee on Disarmament on the eve of the General Assembly's meeting in which this resolution was adopted, may perhaps serve to clarify the significance of the definitions incorporated therein:

> The conclusion is inescapable that the result of the experts' laborious efforts constitutes certain proof of the imperative need for the General Assembly to intervene directly in this matter in order to decide and define, once and for all, certain basic questions relating to the question under consideration. If the experts' exercise in dialectic had produced no other result than this—and, of course, it has produced some others that are not to be disdained—it would alone be sufficient to entitle them to our gratitude.
>
> Of these basic questions, the two which in our view deserve priority attention from the General Assembly at its thirtieth session are, on the one hand, the formulation and adoption of an internationally valid definition of the concept of "nuclear-weapon-free zone" and,

36

on the other, a declaration spelling out the principal obligations of the nuclear-weapon States towards nuclear-weapon-free zones and the States forming such zones.

In this way, the Assembly would be making an effective contribution to the establishment, in the matter under consideration, of some basic norms of international law so frequently invoked in the study of the Ad Hoc Group by some of its members who seem to forget that, since the matter is not only new but very new, inasmuch as the hecatombs of Hiroshima and Nagasaki occurred a bare 30 years ago, such norms of that law as might be applicable to it are either as yet non-existent or still in an embryonic stage. What is more, those norms will have to be developed with the genuine participation of all States and not, as in the nineteenth century, of an insignificant number of States. Hence the intervention of the United Nations in this case would be doubly valuable.[8]

There is no doubt that the two definitions put forth by the General Assembly are of enormous importance in surmounting artificial obstacles to and promoting the establishment of nuclear-weapon-free zones.[9] Thus it seems appropriate to analyze briefly the content of these terms. Since, in addition, the Treaty of Tlatelolco and its two additional protocols conform totally to the norms of those definitions, we will also add a brief account of the most pertinent provisions of this treaty in terms of its meaning and scope.

The definition of what may be considered a "nuclear-weapon-free zone" includes the following elements:

A minimum of two states who "in free exercise of their sovereignty" agree to a treaty or convention, whereby:

a) the statute of total absence of nuclear arms to which the zone will be subject, including the procedures for the delineation of the zone, is defined;

b) an international system of verification and control is established to guarantee compliance with the obligations deriving from that statute; and

c) the General Assembly of the United Nations shall recognize said zone as a nuclear-weapon-free zone.

The form in which these concepts were applied in the Treaty of Tlatelolco, prior to their formulation in the General Assembly, illustrates the point, and it is well to remember how that same assembly recognized the status of a nuclear-weapon-free zone in establishing the Treaty of Tlatelolco.

Sovereign capacity, or "free exercise of sovereignty," necessarily implies that no state may obligate another to form part of a militarily denuclearized zone against its wishes, nor may any state prevent another from becoming part of such a zone if it so desires. This problem was tightly linked to entry into force of the Treaty of Tlatelolco, the issue provoking perhaps the greatest discussion in the Preparatory Commission for the Denuclearization of Latin America (COPREDAL), which accomplished all the preparatory work for the Treaty. When the Preparatory Commission first considered this subject in April of 1966, two distinct trends were manifested. According to the first, the Treaty should go into effect between states which would ratify it on the date of deposit of their respective instruments of ratification, in keeping with the standard practice. The representative Latin American body which would be established by the Treaty should begin its functions as soon as eleven instruments of ratification were deposited, as this number constitutes a majority of the twenty-one members of the Preparatory Commission. Those states supporting the alternative view, on the other hand, argued that the Treaty, although signed and ratified by all member states of the Preparatory Commission, should enter into force only upon the completion of four requirements, essentially those outlined in Article 28 of the Treaty, which may be summarized as follows: the signature and ratification of the Treaty of Tlatelolco and Additional Protocols I and II by all states to which they may be applicable and the conclusion of bilateral or multilateral agreements on the application of the Safeguards System of the International Atomic Energy Agency by all signatory parties to the Treaty and to Additional Protocol I.

As in the course of the third session it was impossible to find solutions to the problems created by these divergent tendencies, the Preparatory Commission incorporated into its proposal of May 3, 1966, two parallel texts. These texts stated respectively the provisions that the Treaty would contain, according to whether one accepted the first or second thesis. To resolve the problem, the co-ordinating committee in its report of December 28, 1966, suggested the adoption of a conciliatory formula, which could receive the approval of all member states of the commission without damage to the respective position of any on the alternative texts.[10] It was this formulation, with some modifications, which was finally to be adopted and incorporated into Article 28 of the Treaty. In keeping with it, the Treaty would go into effect for all signatory states upon the completion of the four requirements specified in paragraph one of the article. That notwithstanding, as the second paragraph of the article suggests,

All signatory states shall have the imprescriptible right to waive, wholly or in part, the requirements laid down in the preceding paragraph. They may do so by means of a declaration which shall be annexed to their respective instrument of ratification and which may be formulated at the time of the deposit of the instrument or subsequently. For those states which exercise this right, this Treaty shall enter into force upon deposit of the declaration, or as soon as those requirements have been met which have not been expressly waived.

The third paragraph of the same article stipulates, moreover:

As soon as this Treaty has entered into force in accordance with the provisions of paragraph 2 for eleven States, the Depositary Government shall convene a preliminary meeting of those States in order that the Agency may be set up and commence its work.

As one can see, an eclectic system was adopted, which at the same time respected the viewpoints of all signatory parties but nonetheless prevented any particular party from being able to preclude the enactment of the Treaty for those states which would voluntarily wish to submit to the statute of military denuclearization defined and developed therein.

Regarding the stability of the zone's limits, the adoption of the procedure which would bring the Treaty into effect had as a consequence two possible interpretations of the term "zone of application": one entailing a moveable zone, in constant progression, and the other a fixed, defined zone. These different concepts are outlined, respectively, in paragraphs one and two of Article 4 of the Treaty. The first of these paragraphs, establishing that "the zone of application of the Treaty is the whole of the territories for which the Treaty is in force" is that which has been used until the present, and, according to what was therein contemplated, the extension and population of the zone has grown gradually as the number of contracting states has increased.

In the second paragraph it is stated that, "upon fulfillment of the requirements of Article 28, paragraph 1, the zone of application of this Treaty shall also be that which is situated in the western hemisphere within the following limits." Such limits are defined according to a series of geographical co-ordinates that can be easily consulted in the Treaty. It suffices to say that, on the one hand, a zone so defined includes considerable areas of the high seas which, in the western part of South America, extend to hundreds of kilometers from the coasts, without naturally implying some pretension of sovereignty or jurisdiction over these sectors. Moreover, in light of the fact that the northern-most loxodromic line of the zone corresponds to 35 degrees north latitude, the paragraph in which it is explained expressly excepts the continental part of the territory of the United States and its territorial waters, which, had that not been specified, would have been included in the Latin American nuclear-weapon-free zone, given that it reaches south of the parallel mentioned above.

Article 1 of the Treaty, which deals with the total absence of nuclear weapons, is written in such clear and unambiguous language that it can bear no other interpretation than banning into perpetuity all nuclear arms from the territories of the contracting parties, regardless of the influence or control other states may try to exercise over them. Thus, the obligations defined in this article are so precise and complete that they leave open no possibility of misinterpretation. According to the stipulations of the article, the contracting parties undertake "to use exclusively for peaceful purposes the nuclear material and facilities which are under their jurisdiction" and "to prohibit and prevent in their respective jurisdictions the testing, use, manufacture, production, or acquisition, by any means whatsoever of any nuclear weapons by the Parties themselves, directly or indirectly, on behalf of anyone else or in any other way." The parties also promise to abstain from "the receipt, storage, installation, deployment, and any form of possession of any nuclear weapons, directly or indirectly, by the Parties themselves, or by any one in their behalf or in any other way."

An international system of verification and control, such as that foreseen in the General Assembly's definition, is established in Articles 13 to 18 of the Treaty. The provisions of these articles constitute—as the then secretary general of the United Nations, U Thant, so aptly pointed out upon the approval of the Treaty in 1967—the first example of the inclusion in an international disarmament agreement of a system of effective control that has its own organs for permanent supervision. The system includes, in effect, the full application of the International Atomic Energy Agency Safeguards System, but has also a much greater range. On the one hand, verification is intended not only to make sure that "devices, services, and facilities intended for peaceful uses of nuclear energy are not used in the testing or manufacture of nuclear weapons" but also to prevent these prohibited activites from being carried out in the territory of the contracting parties with nuclear materials or weapons introduced from abroad.

Moreover, the Treaty grants important controlling functions to the three principal organizations of the Agency for the Prohibition of Nuclear Weapons in Latin America (OPANAL), including the General Conference, the Council and the Secretariat. It provides also for the presentation by the member states of periodic and special reports, the eventual fulfillment of special inspections, and the transmission of reports on the results of such inspections to the Security Council and the General Assembly of the United Nations.

The U.N. General Assembly's recognition that a particular zone should be considered a nuclear-weapon-free zone constitutes the best defense of the legitimate interests of the nations of the Third World. A declaration to this effect from the international organization which is the voice of mankind's conscience will shatter any capricious and self-interested objections that may come in the future from members of the military blocs, and especially from one of the superpowers that sponsor them.

It will be for the General Assembly to decide in each case the specific form it finds appropriate to structure its declaration of recognition of the status of a nuclear-weapon-free zone. It seems worthwhile to remember that in the case of the Latin American zone, the first and, unfortunately, until now the only one covering a densely populated region that has full legal effect, the General Assembly expressed its recognition of the zone's establishment with extraordinary enthusiasm. As resolution 2286 of December 5, 1967, emphatically declared:

> *Welcomes with special satisfaction* the Treaty for the Prohibition of Nuclear Weapons in Latin America, which constitutes an event of historic significance in the efforts to prevent the proliferation of nuclear weapons and to promote international peace and security and which at the same time establishes the right of Latin American countries to use nuclear energy for demonstrated peaceful purposes in order to accelerate the economic and social development of their peoples.

With respect to the second U.N. definition, as already noted, the three principal obligations which pertain to the nuclear-weapon states are the same as those incorporated in 1967 in the first three articles of Additional Protocol II of the Treaty to which four of the five nuclear powers are already parties. The invariable and constant practice of the General Assembly, begun with its resolution 2286 and continued through seven other resolutions, all adopted unanimously and many by more than one hundred votes in favor, has been to advocate without reservation the acceptance of these obligations by nuclear-weapon states.[11] The content of the second paragraph of the definition, which specifies that the obligations in every case should be included in "an international agreement with full juridical power, as a treaty, convention, or protocol, that should be signed and ratified by all nuclear-weapon states," likewise reflects the thesis that the General Assembly has sustained year after year since the approval of resolution 2456 in 1968.

It is well to remember also that, although the General Assembly has focused on the particular importance of the co-operation of nuclear-weapon states since first addressing this question, it has always been careful to avoid suggesting that this cooperation is an indispensable condition for the existence of nuclear-weapon-free zones—which would, in effect, be equivalent to granting nuclear-weapon nations the right to veto. Thus, the General Assembly has, without a doubt, always been quite careful in the selection of the terms used in its resolutions on this subject, mentioning the cooperation of the nuclear-weapon nations as only an element "for the greater efficacy of whatever treaty should establish a nuclear-weapon-free zone."[12]

There are thus solid bases by which to affirm that the Treaty of Tlatelolco and the two definitions of the fundamental concepts relating to the nuclear-weapon-free zones which the General Assembly defined in 1975 have all served to dispel the myth that for the establishment of such zones one must necessarily require that from the beginning all states within the region form part of that zone. It has become clear that although no state can require another to join such a zone, neither can one prevent others wishing to do it from adhering to a regime of total absence of nuclear weapons within their respective territories. Without a doubt, this constitutes a step of incalculable importance to promote new efforts toward the creation of nuclear-weapon-free zones and to fortify recent undertakings in the field.

The example of Tlatelolco, on the other hand, has shown the crucial importance of preparatory *ad hoc* efforts, such as those functions fulfilled for two years by the Preparatory Commission, in attaining the final goal. In a recent study on the projected African nuclear-weapon-free zone, a former director of the U.N. Division of Disarmament, William Epstein, places special emphasis on the importance of this subject, and concludes that, with the establishment of a preparatory commission, the African countries will have won half the battle to denuclearize their continent.[13] Another specialist with experience in the Pacific, Roderic Alley, also reaches conclusions favorable to the viability of a nuclear-weapon-free zone in that region.[14] In light of the value of the precedent set by the Treaty of Tlatelolco, and in view of the General Assembly's definitions, it is to be hoped that the other two nuclear-free-zone projects on the General Assembly's agenda, the Middle East and Southeast Asia, may become equally attainable.

It has already been emphasized that the establishment of nuclear-weapon-free zones constitutes one of the most effective means toward disarmament for nations which do not yet possess these terrible instruments of mass destruction. It seems fitting, in conclusion, to stress that the non-nuclear-weapon states, in face of the superpowers' rejection of authentic efforts towards disarmament, seem inclined to resort to procedures like those applied in the case of an epidemic, i.e., to strengthen the efforts to broaden the zones of the world in which nuclear weapons are proscribed until the territories of those states which are obstinate in possessing them constitute something like a contaminated island, subject to a regimen of quarantine.

Notes

1. The term "disarmament" is used here as in various U.N. forums, to include all kinds of measures related to the prevention, limitation, reduction or elimination of weapons.

2. See U.N. Secretariat, *The United Nations and Disarmament 1945-1970*, pp. 336-355.

3. Alfonso Garcia Robles, in *U.N. General Assembly Official Record (GAOR) (XVIII)*, First Committee, Meeting 1333, November 11, 1963. See also Leopold Benites Vinueza, Representative of Ecuador, *GAOR (XVIII)*, First Committee, Meeting 1328, November 5, 1963:

> The capacity of signing bilateral or multilateral agreements belongs exclusively to States; the sole limitation is that imposed by Article 103 of the Charter. The United Nations has no tutelary power over States; rather it has the moral obligation to assist States in fulfilling the purposes and principles of the Charter, recommending any agreements that might alleviate international tensions and avoid the danger of widening conflicts.

4. The Treaty of Tlatelolco and the two Additional Protocols are reproduced as Appendix IV. For a look at its origins, objectives and results, see Alfonso Garcia Robles, *El Tratado de Tlatelolco,* El Colegio de Mexico, 1967, and *La Proscripcion de las Armas Nucleares en la America Latina,* Mexico, El Colegio Nacional, 1975. The number of contracting parties to the treaty has now reached twenty-two; its Additional Protocol I has been signed and ratified by two of the four states which can be parties to it: the United Kingdom and the Netherlands. President Carter signed Protocol I on behalf of the United States on May 26, 1977. Additional Protocol II has become legally binding upon four—the United Kingdom, the United States, France and China—of

the five nuclear powers to which the General Assembly has directed its exhortations since 1967.

5. Alfonso Garcia Robles, *U.N. General Assembly Official Record (GAOR) (XXX)* Addendum 27A, comments in the Conference of the Committee on Disarmament on receipt of the experts' report:

> First and foremost, among the decisions which we hope the General Assembly will ultimately incorporate in the resolution it adopts in connection with its consideration of the experts' reports should be one which gives an authorized international definition — invocable against both Montagues and Capulets — of the meaning and scope of the concept of "nuclear-weapon-free zone."
>
> The urgent need for such a definition by the Assembly is all too apparent, in view of the content of the experts' study and more particularly of Chapter III, which deals specifically with this aspect of the subject. In it, at every turn, the reader meets with more or less disguised attempts by some Governments to discourage or restrict the establishment of nuclear-weapon-free zones. It talks of an essential requirement — "Where suitable conditions exist for the creation of 'such zones' " — and a little later the word "appropriate" is used; we are told that "several experts pointed out there may be regions in which nuclear-weapon-free zones are impracticable or where their creation may not improve the security of the States of the area"; the chapter adds that "it was argued by some experts that the reduction of tensions must precede the creation of a truly effective nuclear-weapon-free zone"; and we are allowed to share the fruits of the meditations of other members of the *Ad Hoc* Group who argued that "nuclear-weapon-free zones may not be appropriate in all areas."
>
> Truly, we cannot conceal our astonishment at these scruples reflected in the study transmitted to us. We fail to understand why our world, which in 1944, was one gigantic nuclear-weapon-free zone down to the last square meter of its enormous surface, must now, in the very middle of the so-called "disarmament decade," be divided not only into the territories of States having nuclear weapons and that of States without those terrible instruments of mass destruction, but also within the territory occupied by the latter, into areas which have and those which do not have "suitable" conditions in order for the establishment of nuclear-weapon-free zones to be "appropriate."
>
> Who, we wonder, will be called upon to judge such "suitability" or "appropriateness"?

6. U.N. resolution 3261 F (GAOR XXIX) of December 9, 1974.

7. See Appendix V for text of the resolution.

8. *Verbatim Record of the Conference of the Committee on Disarmament, CCD/PV 682* paragraphs 38-40.

9. In the U.N. General Assembly's thirtieth session in 1975, four proposals were made for the creation of nuclear-weapon-free zones, in Africa, the Middle East, South Asia and the South Pacific.

10. The Coordinating Committee of the Preparatory Commission was composed of the president of COPREDAL, its two vice presidents and the three presidents of the working groups created by the Commission.

11. U.N. resolutions: 2666 (GAOR XXV) of December 7, 1970; 2830 (GAOR XXVI) of December 6, 1971; 2935 GAOR XXVII) of November 29, 1972;

3079 (GAOR XXVIII) of December 6, 1973; 3258 (GAOR XXIX) of December 9, 1974; 3467 (GAOR XXX) of December 11, 1975; and 31/67 of December 10, 1976.

12. U.N. resolutions: 1911 (GAOR XVIII) of November 27, 1963; 2286 (GAOR XXII) of December 5, 1967; 2666 (GAOR XXV) of December 7, 1970; 2830 (GAOR XXVI) of December 16, 1971; 2935 (GAOR XXVII) of November 29, 1972; 3079 (GAOR XXVIII) of December 6, 1973; 3258 (GAOR XXX) of December 9, 1974; 3467 (GAOR XXX) of December 11, 1975, and 31/67 of December 10, 1976.

13. William Epstein, *A Nuclear-Weapon-Free Zone in Africa?* The Stanley Foundation, Occasional Paper 14, 1977, pp.23-24.

14. Roderic Alley, *Nuclear-Weapon-Free Zones: The South Pacific Proposal*, The Stanley Foundation, Occasional Paper 14, 1977, pp. 40-43.

International Restraints on Conventional Arms Transfers

Andrew J. Pierre

The transfer of conventional arms to developing countries has become a crucial dimension of the diffusion of power now under way around the globe. The annual rate of worldwide arms transfers, as measured in *deliveries* already made, grew from $3.8 billion in 1965 to $9.7 billion in 1975.[1] These figures give only an incomplete indication of the magnitude of the trend, however, as they do not reflect the enormous increase in *sales* since 1974. U.S. foreign military sales grew from less than a billion in 1970 to $10.6 billion in 1974 and have stayed near the $10 billion mark since then. This American upsurge has been matched by a tripling of arms exports by France and Britain. Total world arms transfers in 1977 alone was above $20 billion.

One cause for the recent massive upsurge of arms sales is quite clear: the new wealth of the oil producing nations and the need for the industrialized, oil consuming countries to find ways to offset, in their balance of payments, the quintupling of the price of oil following the Middle East war of 1973. Yet more fundamental processes are also at work, so that even if the purchase of arms by the Persian Gulf states tapers off, the trend toward the proliferation of conventional arms is likely to continue.

The causes of the diffusion of power are multiple and interrelated. Among the major contributing factors in the dispersion of *political* power are the erosion of bipolarity, the abandon-

47

ment of containment in Asia, and the growth in importance of regional states such as Brazil, Indonesia, Nigeria and Iran. In addition, the new importance of raw materials and basic commodities in a world of increasing competition for natural resources, and the continuing demand for a new economic order, are leading toward a diffusion of *economic* power. *Military* power is being diffused, not only through the steady growth of national defense arsenals and the renewed trend toward nuclear proliferation, but also as a consequence of an increased concern for regional balances and security.

In addition to the *quantitative* increase in arms transferred, there has been a significant *qualitative* increase in the technology of the weapons delivered. In the past the arms transferred, particularly to the developing countries, were often second generation or obsolete weapons of the major powers. Today, many of the arms being sold are among the latest, most advanced weapons available, such as the F-14 and the F-16 fighter aircraft, the TV-guided air-to-ground Maverick missile, and the *Spruance* class destroyers. Some of the most expensive, sophisticated weapons, such as the F-16 fighter, or the AWACS (airborne warning and control system) aircraft if approved, are to be transferred at the same time that they first become available.

Another new trend involves the identity and nature of the recipients. In most of the post-war period, the large proportion of arms transferred went to NATO or Warsaw Pact allies. Today, the dominant portion of transfers is going to the non-industrialized, developing countries. One should not assume that these countries will act less responsibly, but it must also be recognized that the arms being sold to the Middle East, South Asia, and Africa are going to volatile areas where armed conflict is more likely, if for no other reason than the balance of nuclear deterrence which applies to the East-West equation is not present.

It is difficult not to conclude that the large-scale transfer of conventional arms now in progress is being undertaken with few serious restraints and inadequate concern for the long-term impact of the transfers on future prospects for peace. There is little evidence that the principal arms suppliers have adequately weighed the arguments favoring arms sales—for example, for the purpose of improving balance of payments, or of enhancing political leverage—against the reasons for restricting arms transfers because of their consequences for regional stability or for economic development in the recipient countries. Similarly, the recipient countries often do not have a convincing case for diverting scarce economic resources to the purchase of arms. Too often the alleged security requirements for arms are little more than a rationalization for the interest of political or military leaders in acquiring the latest, most sophisticated arms for reasons of prestige or domestic politics.

The Uncertain Benefits of Arms Transfers

Sound judgments about arms transfers are difficult to reach. Unlike the spread of nuclear weapons, there is no global consensus that the transfer of conventional arms is, in every instance, a detriment to the interest of international peace or security. There are no "simple truths" to serve as guidelines for policymakers. Prospective arms transfers may or may not be a stabilizing factor within a region; they may or may not promote the broader foreign policy objectives of the suppliers or the recipients; they may or may not have economic or technological benefits for the seller or the purchaser. Each arms transfer decision has distinct and unique features.

The rationales given for supplying arms sometimes seems appealing but, on closer examination, they are often of ambiguous and uncertain validity, especially when applied to specific cases.

Arms Supplies as Political Influence?

The claim is often made that arms transfers provide political influence for the supplier in relations with the receiving nation. Arms transfers are seen as a symbol of close support and friendly contacts, as giving substance to treaty commitments, and as providing access to political and military elites. The latter benefit has often been cited in the case of arms transfers to Latin America, where most governments are now run by military leaders. For the Soviet Union, political influence has been an important motivation in transferring arms to the Middle East. Similarly, the United States has used arms transfers to gain leverage over sensitive decisions, as in the case of the 1975 Sinai Agreement, when arms were offered to make difficult political or territorial compromises more acceptable.

The nature of such influence can, however, be quite transitory. The United States used its arms relationship with success in deterring a war between Greece and Turkey in 1967, but in 1974 it was powerless to prevent Turkey's invasion of Cyprus. Implicit in the provision of arms by the western powers to Iran has been the belief that such arms transfers will make it less likely that the Shah will support an Arab embargo cutting off the supply of oil, but the fact is that Iran has been a leader within the Organization of Petroleum Exporting Countries (OPEC) and until recently, at least, has been arguing for higher oil prices. The experience of the Soviet Union in Egypt is further evidence of the transitory nature of "influence." Close ties were developed between the two countries when an arms agreement was reached in 1955, and after the 1967 Mid-East war Moscow gained the use of naval facilities in Alexandria for its Mediterranean fleet. Yet Sadat expelled Soviet leaders in 1972 and after the Yom Kippur war changed the orientation of Egypt's foreign policy toward closer ties with the West.

Indeed, the aim of influence through arms can lead to a "reverse leverage" by the recipient over the supplier. This is particularly true with arms that have been granted in exchange for base rights, as in Turkey or the Philippines; but more generally, the supplier-recipient ties can lead to a symbiotic relationship which limits the freedom of both. For example, the United States cannot now abandon its arms transfer commitments to Iran without a major crisis in Washington-Tehran relations. If Iran were to become involved in a war, it might be difficult to keep some of the 24,000 American personnel there uninvolved, and the risks exist that they might become "hostage" at a time of crisis.[2]

Arms Supplies to Fulfill Security Needs of Recipients?

A second cluster of rationales for supplying arms is to help fulfill the security requirements of recipient countries and to increase regional stability. From the early post-war period until the 1970s, when most arms transfers were in the form of military grants rather than sales, this was the fundamental reason for the U.S. transmission of arms to NATO and other allies such as Japan. The Nixon Doctrine expanded the reliance upon arms transfers by emphasizing the giving of U.S. arms to indigenous forces as a replacement for American military personnel stationed abroad.

Although the transfer of arms may serve to create a balance within a region, it may equally create an arms race which could be destabilizing. The large-scale transfers to Iran and Saudi Arabia are justified as enhancing regional security. But within the region, they are viewed by many in competitive terms. Saudi Arabia may not think of itself as needing to "balance" Iran militarily, but for reasons of prestige and politics it does want to have equal access to arms. Such arms, once acquired, must then be counted as part of the Arab-Israeli military balance, since weapons sent to Saudi Arabia could be retransferred to one of the confrontation states. An arms-race dynamic can be seen in other regions such as South Asia; between India and Pakistan; Latin America, where Brazil and Argentina as well as Peru and Chile acquire arms in a competitve manner; and East Africa, where Idi Amin has imported Soviet arms and thereby forced Tanzania and Kenya to build up their capabilities. Arms transfers in themselves do not necessarily create conflict, but their availability increases the chance of a military response to a political dispute, and a particularly rapid infusion of arms into a region may have a highly destabilizing effect. If a war should start, the larger number and more sophisticated nature of arms acquired from abroad can make the conflict more destructive, increasing the chances of escalation by outside powers.

Recently, a new strategic rationale has been given for arms transfers. With the increasing risk of nuclear proliferation, the provision of conventional arms, some contend, can be used to reduce the incentive for non-nuclear countries to acquire a nuclear weapons capability. Arms sales to Pakistan have been justified in order to dissuade that country from becoming a nuclear power. The same justifications have been made with regard to South Korea and Israel.

This argument is of doubtful validity. If a nation were to perceive its security so threatened that it had to have, for deterrence purposes, an independent nuclear capability, it would be unlikely to be dissuaded by an uncertain supply of conventional weapons from abroad. Moreover, in most countries a decision to acquire nuclear weapons is likely to be made for a number of reasons in addition to security, such as prestige, regional dominance, scientific and military interests, or the pressures of domestic politics. In these circumstances, conventional arms are unlikely to be perceived as viable alternatives. On the contrary, the acquisition of new, sophisticated arms is more likely to whet the appetites of military and political leaders for nuclear weapons.

Economic Benefits for Arms Suppliers?

Arms sales are often viewed as an important source of foreign exchange, contributing to a more favorable balance of payments. They provide employment in the defense industry and create economies of scale, thereby reducing per-unit costs of arms manufactured for the armed forces of the supplier country. Such considerations are not unimportant in the United States and, to a lesser degree, the Soviet Union, but they are much more critical for European producers, which have a far smaller domestic market for arms and whose defense industries are therefore more dependent upon overseas sales.

51

The economic significance of arms sales can, however, be exaggerated. Only 3.5% of France's total exports in 1975 were in the form of arms exports and they accounted for only one-fifth of the exports to the oil-producing countries of the Middle East. Of a total work force of 22 million, only 70,000 are engaged in manufacturing weapons for customers abroad. Roughly comparable figures apply to Britain.

The maintenance of viable national defense industries is perceived as an important political goal, especially in France, where it is linked with notions of dependence and sovereignty, but to a lesser extent also in Britain. However, this must be seen in the context of strong economic and technological pressures created by the rising costs of arms and defense which are gradually driving the Europeans toward greater weapons cooperation among themselves and across the Atlantic.

In the United States, foreign military sales account for 4% of total exports and provide employment for an estimated 300,000 workers, or less than half of one percent of total employment. The Congressional Budget Office has estimated that the savings generated through enlarged production runs and recoupment of research and development costs in a program of $8 billion arms sales per year comes to $560 million.[3] This amounts to roughly .005% of the 1977 defense budget. Comparable data is not available for the Soviet Union, but we know that in its policy of granting long-term, low-interest loans to arms purchasers, the U.S.S.R. has traditionally emphasized the political significance rather than the economic benefits of arms sales. In none of the main suppliers, therefore, do arms exports occupy as important a role in their national economies as is often assumed by those who believe that economic imperatives must overrule any attempts to restrain arms sales.

The United Nations as a Vehicle for Restraint?

Despite the global nature of the arms trade phenomenon (with probably every country in the world purchasing some arms abroad) and the obvious significance of the problem for international peace and security, the United Nations has failed thus far to make much progress in dealing with the arms trade question.

The League of Nations published from 1925 until 1938 an annual statistical yearbook on the trade in arms and ammunitions. The suggestion is sometimes made, most recently by Alva Myrdal, that such a yearbook be undertaken by the United Nations.[4] Although this would do no harm, neither would it necessarily do much good. The assumption appears to be that greater public awareness and exposure of the arms trade through publication will create pressures which will force governments to limit arms sales. Unfortunately, there is little evidence that this assumption is valid.

Within the United Nations, four attempts have been made to deal with the arms trade. All were unsuccessful. In 1965, Malta proposed that the Eighteen Nation Committee on Disarmament consider the question of arms transfers with the view of submitting to the General Assembly proposals for giving greater attention to the problem. Denmark, in 1967, suggested that the secretary general make an inquiry concerning the views of member states on arms trade legislation. In 1970, Sweden and the United Kingdom raised the subject of the arms trade at the Geneva Committee on Disarmament. The fourth, and most recent, attempt occurred in 1976 at the thirty-first U.N. General Assembly when the foreign ministers of six countries (Japan, Belgium, Ireland, the Netherlands, the Philippines, and Singapore) devoted a major part of their addresses to the question of the conventional arms race. These six delegations, joined by eight relatively small countries (Ghana, Liberia, Colombia, Denmark, Bolivia, El Salvador, Norway, and New Zealand), co-sponsored a draft resolution requesting the secretary general to undertake a factual study of the problem and to solicit the views of member states.[5] This proposal, like the three before it, was defeated. It was opposed by many of the larger countries of the Third World, namely Argentina, Algeria, Brazil, India, Mexico, Nigeria, and Yugoslavia.

In retrospect, failure of even these modest U.N. efforts to address the arms trade phenomenon relates primarily to perceptions of a majority of the Third World countries, many of which regard the proposals as embarrassing and divisive of the non-aligned group. Moreover, they were seen as discriminatory in that they appeared to focus more on the responsibilities of the recipients than the suppliers.

Nevertheless, there are a number of reasons, as already noted, why purchasing countries may see some advantages in restraints on the transfer of arms into their region. Internationally accepted controls on arms transfers can become a way of preventing regional arms races or precluding the spending of limited financial resources on military weapons rather than on economic and social development. Perhaps the strongest condemnation of unrestrained arms *imports* was voiced in a speech before the thirty-first session of the U.N. General Assembly by S. Rajaratnam, the foreign minister of Singapore:

> The massive flow of arms to the Third World confronts it with a new danger. It is first of all a drain on

their economies. But even more important is the fact that it creates a new form of dependence on the Great Powers who can exploit the Third World's dependence on them for arms, to manipulate them, to engineer conflicts between them, and to use them as proxies in their competition for influence and dominance.[6]

The U.N. Special Session on Disarmament need not adopt such a radical perspective successfully to point out some of the disadvantages of the present proliferation of arms transfers. By focusing world attention on the question it may give new impetus to efforts to restrain arms transfers. Such controls are more likely to be agreed upon at the regional than the universal or U.N. level. The principal task of the Special Session may therefore be educational, but the advantages of this should not be minimized. A new climate of international opinion will need to be created if significant reductions are to be achieved. The Special Session can make a major contribution to the development of new perspectives on arms transfers and to the infusion of a greater sense of urgency in dealing with the problem. Beyond this, what can be achieved at the United Nations remains somewhat limited.

Supplier-Initiated Restraints

Given the difficulties which exist in dealing with the arms trade at the universal level, the best opportunities for progress may exist within smaller groupings—among the principal supplier countries and among the recipient countries within a geographical region. Most discussions at the Conference of the Committee on Disarmament have assumed that the initiative must come from the recipient states within a region. Although this should be attempted whenever possible, a more realistic and fruitful approach may lie in cooperative regulation among the supplier countries.

If one takes as a standard of measurement the export of major arms such as aircraft, missiles, naval vessels, and armored fighting vehicles, the number of countries which export such arms to the developing world in significant quantities is only four. The United States (36%), the Soviet Union (34%), France (10%), and Britain (10%) exported 90% of the major weapons transferred to the developing world in 1975.[7] When one adds a few members of the NATO alliance (West Germany, Canada, Italy, the Netherlands) as well as the Soviet Union's Warsaw Pact ally, Czechoslovakia, the figure is raised to 95%. The fifth largest exporter is West Germany, but its transfers to the Third World are still one-fourth those of France or Britain.

The largest supplier not included in one of the two alliances is the People's Republic of China, but it accounts for slightly less than one percent of arms transfers to developing countries. Although there are a number of countries which are developing indigenous arms industries, such as Israel, South Africa, India, Taiwan, and Brazil, they are not likely to export sufficient quantities in the next decade to have a major impact on the international arms trade. Sophisticated weapons require skilled labor and engineering knowledge; while simpler weapons may be increasingly manufactured by indigenous industries, Third World countries will continue to import most sophisticated items.

This pattern of production suggests the possibility of some form of cooperation among the Big Four if the political objectives of such cooperation, however loosely defined, can be agreed upon. These countries have an established history of joint involvement in East-West arms control negotiations and intra-alliance diplomacy. To bring them together on the problem of conventional arms transfers, though difficult, would by no means be impossible.

As an initial step, the major suppliers might seek to establish criteria by which to regulate those arms transfers which would have a destabilizing influence within a region; for example, subjecting to restraint, those sales which could:

- create an imbalance which upsets an existing balance;
- feed a local arms race;
- foster instability because of the sudden acquisition of new arms;
- provide incentives for a surprise attack;
- provide incentives for a pre-emptive action;
- quicken the pace and scale of escalation;
- introduce more destructive arms into a region;
- introduce starkly inhuman weapons into a region; and
- provide weapons which might be used internally in civil war, police action, or violation of human rights.

Restraints might be qualitative, quantitative, or geographical. In practice, there would be a combination of these. Although some qualitative restraints might be worldwide, many of the qualitative and perhaps all the quantitative restraints might be regional or national. Among the *qualitative* restraints which might be considered would be:

- surface-to-surface missiles above a certain range;

- dual-purpose weapons that could deliver nuclear as well as non-nuclear warheads;

- arms apt to be employed by terrorists, such as the shoulder-fired Redeye missile;

- attack submarines;

- aircraft carriers;

- advanced fighter-bomber aircraft;

- precision-guided munitions;

- inhuman weapons, such as concussion bombs;

- highly destructive weapons designed for essentially offensive purposes; and

- weapons that could inflict large-scale damage on population centers.

Similarly, *quantitative* restraints could be developed according to the need to maintain or create a balance within a region. Quantitative restraints might involve:

- overall arms ceilings within a region;

- the maintenance of a prescribed ratio of arms among states within a region;

- limits on the arms possessed by a country; and

- permissible rates of replacement.

Many other aspects of the arms trade phenomenon might be dealt with cooperatively among the supplier countries, such as agreements on the re-transfer of weapons or on licensing and co-production arrangements. Whatever the eventual form of joint regulation, the most promising opportunities are likely to be restraints on the transfer of sophisticated, highly destructive technologies to particular geographical regions.

Recipient-Initiated Restraints

Contrary to the conventional wisdom, restraints among the supplier countries may be the most promising approach to developing some workable international control over the arms trade. Nevertheless regional arms control arrangements, or zones of limited armaments, negotiated within an area are potentially very important. This has already been attempted with somewhat limited, but not insignificant, success in Latin America among the Andean states in the Declaration of Ayacucho, signed in 1974. The still relatively small volume of arms transfers to Sub-Saharan Africa provides another opportunity for genuine, regionally-inspired restraints. The most pressing need for multinational restraints exists in the Middle

East and the Persian Gulf regions. Restraints on arms transfers to the Arab-Israel confrontation states might be worked out as part of an overall peace settlement in coordination with the supplier countries. One can imagine a Persian Gulf understanding placing some cap of qualitative and quantitative nature on the current arms build-up in that area.

Recipient states within a geographical zone might set limitations or ceilings on the purchase of certain types of arms. Such limitations would recognize legitimate defense needs but within a regional plan that seeks to avoid an excessive transfer of arms. Qualitative restraints might be especially feasible on weapons which had not been previously introduced into the region.

It is often assumed that purchasing countries do not want to accept any self-restraints on their arms imports. The usual corollary to this is that any restraints set by the suppliers on their exports would be perceived by the recipients as inherently discriminatory and as a somewhat arrogant manifestation of paternalistic attitudes.

Certainly every state has the right to make its own determination of its national security requirements. But this does not negate the possibility that states within a region may find some common purpose in limiting transfers into their area. There are a number of incentives for Third World countries to reduce the inflow of conventional arms. The purchase of weapons may divert scarce economic resources from pressing social and development needs. The availability of arms in massive quantities or of a sophisticated nature may encourage the growth of the influence of the military within a society in undesirable ways. The transfer of arms may create political tensions within a region through the military buildup of a state or through a competitive arms environment leading to an arms race. Accordingly, there may exist a mutuality of interests in preventing the adverse effects of arms transfers upon the existing political and military balance within a region. At least there exists a structure of disincentives, as well as incentives, for receiving arms. The international regulation of arms sales should be potentially attractive to recipients as well as to supplier states.

Ideally, therefore, restraints on arms flows should be agreed upon by both the purchasers and the producers. Recipients can make an important contribution to helping shape the nature of restraints which might be agreed upon by the supplier countries and discussions between purchasers and producers should be encouraged.

The Carter Administration's Initiatives

As the largest exporter of arms, the United States has special responsibility in seeking ways to contain the proliferation of conventional arms. This has been recognized by the Carter administration, which announced on May 19, 1977, a set of guidelines on U.S. arms transfers designed to impose new restraints. According to these guidelines, the United States will view arms transfers as an "exceptional" instrument of foreign policy to be used only in those instances where it can be "clearly demonstrated that the transfer contributes to our national security interests." The United States henceforth, it was stated, (1) will not be the first supplier to introduce into a region newly-developed, advanced weapons which could create a new or significantly higher combat capability; (2) will not permit the development or significant modification of advanced weapon systems solely for the purpose of export; (3) will limit co-production agreements with foreign governments for significant weapons, equipment, and major components; (4) will not allow, as a pre-condition of sales, the re-transfer of certain weapons and equipment to third parties; (5) will impose new regulations requiring government authorization for promoting the sale of arms abroad; and (6) will reduce the dollar volume of new commitments under the Foreign Military Sales and Military Assistance Programs from a ceiling equivalent to the total for fiscal year 1977.

Sufficient flexibility was left in the fine wording of the guidelines to permit exceptions when circumstances appear to require them.[8] The pattern of arms sales during the first ten months of 1977 has demonstrated the difficulties in implementing the Carter administration's guidelines. Washington decided not to sell 250 F-18s to Iran, turned down a request from Pakistan for 110 A-7 attack aircraft, refused to allow Israel to sell Kfir fighter planes equipped with American-built engines to Ecuador, and curtailed military assistance to several countries (Brazil, Argentina, and Uruguay) which were perceived to be violating some human rights provisions in the guidelines. On the other side of the ledger, however, the Carter administration supported the sale of several billion dollars worth of AWACS aircraft to Iran and the transfer of F-15s to Saudi Arabia, suggested sending U.S. technicians to rehabilitate the Egyptian Air Force, and disclosed intended arms sales to Sudan, Chad, and Somalia as well as a $1.86 billion military aid program for South Korea to compensate for the planned withdrawal of U.S. forces. Arms sales for fiscal year 1977 will be at least as high as in recent years.

The difficulties in implementing a policy of restraint, however well-intentioned, are a reminder of the close link between arms sales and foreign policy objectives. Weapons transfer decisions are uncommonly complex, involving a myriad of considerations, and require considerable discrimination and polical sensitivity. Arms control objectives can only succeed when they are reinforced by both general, and country-specific, foreign policy considerations.

It is too early to make a clear judgment on the ultimate outcome of the Carter administration's attempt to impose self-restraints. But there can be little doubt that such restraints will have little chance to succeed over a period of time if they are not matched to some degree by the other supplier countries. The often-heard maxim—"if we do not sell, others will"—has too often been used as an excuse for inaction and has been allowed to engender a sense of futility. Yet it does have considerable validity. For this reason, international cooperation designed to regulate the arms trade is essential if it is to be curtailed.

As the world's leading arms merchant, the United States can and should take the first step. Other major suppliers should now be encouraged to adopt matching restraints. Not only would these have value in themselves, but they would facilitate a firmer adherence by the United States to a policy of restraint. The challenge to the world community is to multi-lateralize the process through supplier, recipient, and supplier-recipient discussions. The U.N. Special Session is especially well-suited to contribute to a new sense of awareness and urgency. It comes, moreover, at an apt time, when a serious effort is being undertaken in the dominant weapons-selling country to restrain its sales. This is the first time this has occurred, and it may well be the last if the spiraling arms trade continues uncontrolled. The challenge before the Special Session is to seize the unique, present momentum so as to help restore moderation to the proliferation of arms transfers.

Notes

1. U.S. Arms Control and Disarmament Agency, *World Military Expenditures and Arms Transfers, 1965-1974, 1966-1975.*

2. These concerns were expressed in a staff report to the Subcommittee on Foreign Assistance, Committee on Foreign Relations, U.S. Senate, July 1976, *U.S. Military Sales to Iran.*

3. Congressional Budget Office, *Budgetary Cost Savings to the Department of Defense Resulting from Foreign Military Sales,* Staff Working Paper, May 24, 1976.

4. Alva Myrdal, *The Game of Disarmament* (New York: Pantheon Books, 1976), p. 145.

5. U.N. General Assembly, 31st Session, First Committee, A/C.1/31/L.20, November 22, 1976.

6. Statement of Mr. S. Rajaratnam, minister for Foreign Affairs of Singapore and chairman of the delegation before the thirty-first session at the U.N. General Assembly, Permanent Mission of Singapore to the United Nations, September 29, 1976.

7. Stockholm International Peace Research Institute, *Yearbook 1976*, p.253.

8. For the full text of the Carter administration's guidelines on U.S. arms transfers see Appendix VI.

Arms and Dependence

Mary Kaldor

The Special Session of the U.N. General Assembly marks a new awareness of the global nature of the arms race. People are beginning to talk about the "new world military order" a nexus of recent events which may cause a profound change in international military relationships. These include the new phase in the strategic arms race, the burgeoning arms trade, and the proliferation of nuclear capabilities. There are also new military technologies, exemplified by the neutron bomb and precision-guided munitions, which narrow the gap between conventional and nuclear forces and alter perceptions of military power in ways that are unpredictable and hence destabilizing.

Viewed from an international perspective, these developments mean a heightened danger of war and further wastage of economic resources. Yet from a national perspective these same developments are often seen as a reason for increased military spending. Increased armament by an opponent is seen to represent a threat to military security. Increased armament by a friendly nation is seen as a political challenge, part of the competition for status within the international system. In particular, non-aligned nations frequently argue that attempts to control the trade in arms without controlling production amounts to discrimination. Third World countries, it is said, must arm at a faster rate than advanced industrial countries if they are to reduce military inequality and to increase political power.

So it is that the international interest in disarmament is counter-poised against the national interest in armament in much the same way that the economic nationalism of the 1930s seemed an insuperable barrier to the creation of a liberal world

61

economy. Since the Special Session is unlikely to produce the conditions for total global agreement on disarmament, it is worth questioning this line of argument. It is worth asking whether there are, in fact, ways of reducing the level of armaments in the absence of international agreement and whether the most positive contribution of next year's Special Session might not be a change in the current climate of gloomy opinion.

The national case for acquiring arms is based on the assumption that military power can be measured by accepted international critera and that political power is directly derived from military power so measured. The criteria for measurement are those that emphasize the importance of the superpowers. By accepting these criteria, it could be said that Third World countries are accepting a dependent ideology. Indeed, one might go further and argue that every attempt to increase political power and national independence on the basis of this ideology in fact results in increased dependence and that the acquisition of armaments is one mechanism whereby Third World countries are drawn into the global confrontation between the superpowers and are incorporated into a world division of labor which limits their full potential for development.

The criteria for measuring military power include such things as the dollar size of military budgets and the quantities of men, tanks and aircraft. Considerable weight is attached to the sophistication and modernity of military equipment, assessed according to the date and type of equipment and to performance characteristics such as speed, payload, or electronic capabilities. A particularly high value is assigned to nuclear weapons. Using such global indicators, one would have had to conclude that the United States enjoyed an overwhelming military superiority over its enemies in Indochina and that the Arabs enjoyed a similar advantage over Israel. But military power, of course, is not about quantities; it is about the ability to achieve specific political or strategic objectives through military means. Even for advanced industrial nations it is not at all clear that the two meanings of military power are compatible, that the sophisticated arsenals of East or West will necessarily prove an advantage in actual battlefield conditions. Improvement in the accuracy and destructiveness of convention munitions suggests that the dispersal tactics of Vietnam may be a more apt precedent than the more orthodox battles of World War II. The increased vulnerability of all weapon platforms—ships, tanks, aircraft—calls into question the utility of equipment which is difficult to hide and expensive to replace. In addition, complex modern equipment entails considerable logistical problems. A squadron of F-4 Phantoms, for example, requires an inventory of 70,000 spare parts to be kept operational under war-time conditions. Despite the unprecedented scale and sophistication of logistical operations in Vietnam, there were perennial shortages.

For Third World countries, such doubts about the military value of modern armaments are magnified. First of all, sophisticated weapons systems are highly capital-intensive, requiring an advanced industrial base for repair, maintenance and operation. The shortage of skilled industrial manpower, the inadequacy of roads and airfields, etc., is bound to impair military efficiency. Indeed, in some cases, equipment confidently accredited to Third World countries actually lies rusting, often uncrated, in ports. There is growing evidence that in the Pakistani wars, where the education and skills of the soldiers were roughly matched, sophisticated military equipment actually proved a handicap.[1] For example, in 1965, Pakistani soldiers were unable to operate the automatic controls needed to fire the guns of their *Patton* tanks, which considerably hampered their offensive. More importantly, perhaps, in the context of this paper, is the fact that the relative scarcity of those factors of production needed to operate a modern military machine adhering to the standards set by advanced industrial countries means that Third World countries are heavily dependent on their suppliers for spare parts and for services. We may note the concern that has been expressed about the growth of "white-collar mercenaries" in various parts of the world.

All this suggests that the acquisition of modern armaments may not contribute to military power in the true sense of the expression. It may be that a clearer focus on military tasks as opposed to military means would result in alternative, possibly labor-intensive solutions. Such an argument would also imply that political power based on the size and sophistication of arsenals is no more than a matter of perception. Indeed, the military dependence induced by the acquisition of modern armaments may actually reduce political power. For example, both the United States and the Soviet Union have been able to use arms supplied to the Middle East as a way of bargaining for short-term diplomatic objectives.[2] This would not be possible if the demand for armaments were less. Furthermore, in wartime, military dependence means that suppliers have the power of military veto. And supplier involvement is the mechanism through which local and particular events are transformed into the substance of global conflict.

The fact that current assumptions about military power are so widely accepted suggests that their significance is more than merely military. If one accepts the connection between beliefs and social setting and its corollary that every society has its own military ideology, then the pervasive nature of modern attitudes towards armament has profound implications for the unity of the international system. Emmanuel Terray has described how the introduction of imported guns transformed society in pre-colonial Africa. It led to the introduction of slavery, alongside a kin-based mode of subsistence production. The slaves were used to produce gold for exports, and the revenue was spent on prestige goods and guns to capture and maintain more slaves. This, he argues, was the origin of the state in pre-colonial West Africa.[3] Likewise, it can be argued that the introduction of modern military technology in Third World countries has a powerful influence on the pattern of industrialization and on political structure.

In the early sixties, it was fashionable to argue that the army as a modern institution could make a positive contribution to industrialization and economic growth in underdeveloped countries.[4] Support for these ideas came from Professor Benoit's attempt to demonstrate, not altogether convincingly, a positive correlation between the share of gross national product devoted to military spending and the rate of growth of civilian gross national product.[5] In recent years, however, people have begun to question whether "modernization," industrialization and economic growth can be said to constitute economic and social development. Indeed, it is argued that economic growth involves increased economic inequality and even perhaps a reduction in the standard of living of the poorest people, that industrialization involves increased foreign dependence, and that modernization, meaning the introduction of modern attitudes and modern technology, may conflict with the satisfaction of basic needs.

The connection between the level of military technology and the level of industrialization is fairly well established. For example, the more industrialized Third World countries like India, Egypt, Argentina, Brazil or South Korea are the ones which possess the most sophisticated armaments and even a rudimentary capacity for the manufacture of arms. For most underdeveloped countries, armaments represent a very high proportion of total capital imports. And in many countries, industrial capacity is reserved for the repair of weapons. Indeed, a recent study by the Hamburg Group on Armaments and Underdevelopment suggests that it is the requirement of the modern industrial army that shapes the whole pattern of industrialization.[6]

It is a capital-intensive pattern of industrialization which is heavily dependent on foreign technology, aid, and investment. This is consistent with other empirical studies. Benoit's finding about the relationship between military spending and economic growth, described above, could be spurious, since high economic growth rates can also be explained by high levels of foreign aid. Similarly, Philippe Schmitter, in a survey of Latin American countries for the period 1950-1967, found that the association between militarism and high rates of economic growth could be more accurately explained by foreign dependence.[7]

It is also a pattern of industrialization that tends to generate inequality. In addition to foreign aid and investment, the foreign exchange and savings needed to finance industrialization are extracted from the production of primary products in the countryside for the world market. The benefits of industrialization are not redistributed but are spent on luxury consumption by the elite, spent on arms, reinvested in further industrialization, repatriated by foreign investors as profits, or returned to aid donors as debt repayment. Because industry is capital intensive, it does not generate sufficient employment to absorb the surplus rural population. Unfortunately, there is very little empirical evidence about economic inequality. The rate of infant mortality could be taken as a rough indicator of the standard of living of the mass of the population. Countries like Brazil, Iran, or South Korea which are characterized by high levels of military spending and by a dependent pattern of industrialization tend to have a rate in infant mortality that is above the regional average.[8]

In a strategy of modernization and industrialization which involves heavy foreign dependence and inequality, arms imports not only reinforce the economic patterns described above, they can produce other effects. First, popular dissatisfaction over inequality may bring on military repression (although, of course, the most sophisticated instrument of the modern industrial army may not be the most appropriate for internal repression). Perhaps more importantly, popular dissatisfaction may preclude the possibility of democratic legitimacy. The import of modern armaments may provide the military with a vested interest in that particular strategy of industrialization, such that elections may be replaced by a military coup, if this strategy were challenged.[9]

If this interpretation is correct, then armaments play a critical role in cementing the current international system; the "world military order" now prevailing serves to uphold current hierarchies of international political and economic relationships. The ideology of political power, based on quantities of armaments, offers Third World nations an opportunity to raise their status within the international system by imitation; yet imitators must, of necessity, always lag behind the imitated. Recognition of this contradiction would be a radical step. Unilateral or regional attempts to reduce the level of arms purchases could be viewed as part of a policy aimed at a new world economic order which furthered full economic and social development. It might mean, for example, a shift in priorities from capital-intensive to labor-intensive technologies, from town to countryside, and from international to local initiatives. Undertaken on a sufficiently wide scale, such a policy would induce a re-examination of the prevailing ideology among advanced industrialized countries. Dependence is not one-sided. The industrialized countries need the markets in the developing world for arms and capital goods and the supplies of primary products; in particular the arms trade has been important in postponing the crisis of the arms industries in Western Europe and the United States.

One important task of the Special Session should be to expose the myth that political power is the inevitable concomitant of national armament. The possibilities for some measure of genuine disarmament would be greatly improved by the idea, whose very acceptance could make it come true, that the power of Third World countries is the power *not* to buy arms.

Notes

1. See *The Arms Trade with the Third World* (Stockholm: Stockholm International Peace Research Institute, 1971), Chapter 16; and Javed Ansari and Mary Kaldor, "Imported Military Technology and Conflict Dynamics: the Bangladesh Crisis of 1971," in the *The New Military World Order: The Transfer of Military Technology from Rich to Poor Countries* (International Peace Research Association, forthcoming).

2. See Leslie Gelb, "Arms Sales," *Foreign Policy,* No. 25, (Winter, 1976-1977).

3. See Emmanuel Terray, "Long Distance Exchange and the Formation of the State: The Case of the Abron Kingdom of Guyaman," *Economy and Society,* Vol. 3, No. 3.

4. Essays on this theme can be found in H. Bienan, ed., *The Military and Modernization* (Chicago: Aldine Atherton, Inc., 1971) and John J. Johnson, *The Role of the Military in Underdeveloped Countries* (Princeton: Rand Corporation, 1972).

5. See Emile Benoit, *Defense and Economic Growth in Developing Countries* (Lexington, Massachusetts: Lexington Books, 1973).

6. See Peter Lock and Herbert Wulf, *Register on Arms Production in Developing Countries* (Hamburg: Study Group on Armaments and Underdevelopment, March, 1977).

7. See P.C. Schmitter, "Military Intervention, Political Competitiveness

and Public Policy in Latin America: 1950-67" in Morris Janowitz and Jack Van Doon, eds., *On Military Intervention* (Rotterdam: Rotterdam University Press, 1971).

8. See M. Kaldor and J.P. Perry Robinson, "War" in M. Jahoda et al., eds., *World Futures: The Great Debate* (Martin Robertson, forthcoming). A discussion of the relationship between inequality and military spending in Brazil by Brazilian Marxist Cardoso can be found in Alfred Stephan, *Authoritarian Brazil: Origins, Policies and Future* (New Haven: Yale University Press, 1973).

9. This argument is elaborated in Mary Kaldor, "The Military in Development," *World Development* (June, 1976).

Monitoring Arms Control
Do We Need a Global Verification Institution?

Jozef Goldblat

Although no direct relationship has been established between the degree of compliance with international treaties and the extent of supervision, governments are generally disinclined to depend solely on good faith, especially when matters of national security are involved.[1] Mutual interests which usually exist at the time a treaty is concluded are no guarantee that pressures will not build up later to bypass the obligations, either in the center of power or in various sectors of political and military establishments. Hence, the problem of possible breaches has been a dominant topic ever since arms control and disarmament became a subject of interstate transactions.

Sovereign governments cannot be prevented from violating international commitments, openly or secretly, if they choose to disregard the consequences of their actions. They may, however, be deterred from doing so, if they are afraid of losing the advantages they have originally gained from the treaty, if they dread an expected or unpredictable response from the injured states, and if they are sufficiently sensitive to public disapproval to apprehend an unfavorable reaction in their own and in other countries. Deterrence of secret violations presupposes the ability to detect them, and timely detection might enable the injured party to redress the situation. This is the primary purpose of verification clauses in arms control and disarmament treaties.

To be meaningful, verification should normally include procedures for acquiring information about the parties' performance with respect to their undertakings, for instituting an inquiry in cases requiring clarification, and for dealing with complaints of violations. A review of twelve post-World War II arms control agreements reveals that the above requirements have been met in a variety of ways.[2]

With regard to acquisition of information, the parties to such treaties as the Antarctic Treaty, the Treaty of Tlatelolco, or the Outer Space Treaty are under an obligation to submit declarations or notifications, as well as regular or special reports on certain activities, or to state the absence of prohibited activities.[3] Pertinent technical data are to be transmitted under the Threshold Test Ban Treaty and the Peaceful Nuclear Explosions Treaty. The right to observe from ground, sea and air, as well as to visit relevant areas or plants, sometimes on the basis of free access, is assured in the Antarctic Treaty, the Sea-Bed Treaty, the Non-Proliferation Treaty, and the Peaceful Nuclear Explosions Treaty. In other cases, knowledge about compliance is gathered solely by so-called national technical means of verification (non-intrusive means of surveillance, such as satellite photography), with an understanding, explicit or implicit, that states will not interfere with the operation of such means.

With regard to problems relating to the application of treaties, most of the arms control agreements considered here provide for clarification through consultation between the parties concerned. This implies cooperation in furnishing replies. In multilateral treaties provision has also been made for consultation through international procedures.

With regard to charges of violation of obligations, with the exception of those deriving from bilateral treaties, complaints are to be lodged with the U.N. Security Council. The Security Council may carry out investigations on the basis of the complaint received and decide whether a violation has occurred. Under the Antarctic Treaty, disputes may be referred to the International Court of Justice for settlement.

In spite of elaborate provisions, the verification procedures embodied in existing treaties suffer from lack of consistency. Checking compliance with arms control obligations often requires the use of sophisticated equipment — reconnaissance satellites, electronic devices, or modern means of transportation — in addition to the more traditional ways of collecting intelligence information. The few nations possessing such resources can rely for the most part on their own national means of verification. However, for nations lacking the wherewithal, the mere right to verify is, to a large extent, meaningless; they may hardly be in a position to ascertain whether the commitments of their partners are being upheld.

The consultation procedure devised to clear up problems relating to the implementation of treaties may be of little use to countries deprived of knowledge about the behavior of others. Moreover, direct, bilateral consultation, though advisable *per se* may not always be feasible. With regard to indirect, international consultation, most treaties use vague language to cover such an eventuality: the procedures must be "appropriate" and placed within the framework of the United Nations in accordance with its charter. If this means the right to approach the United Nations through the usual channels, then the clause is redundant.

Complaints of breaches can be lodged with the U.N. Security Council, but the procedure is inapplicable for agreements among the great powers, which have the right of veto in the Security Council, and may be of little use even under multilateral treaties. Allegations submitted must contain evidence confirming their validity, and a state not possessing such evidence, for lack of reliable information, may have its request for consideration rejected by the Security Council. And even if the Security Council agrees to discuss a charge which does not completely satisfy the above requirement, there is always a danger that the case will not be given proper examination and will remain unresolved: the great-power veto is often perceived to have been used to block not only substantive decisions, but also proposals for investigation or observation, when the interests of the permanent members of the Security Council, or their allies, were involved. Besides, a complainant may find himself in an inconvenient situation if Security Council members not party to a given treaty are called upon to judge the conduct of the parties.[4] In view of these uncertainties, countries may be hesitant to embark on a procedure which extends the inequality of states under the U.N. Charter to relations under arms control agreements. The option left open is to withdraw, if there is an appropriate clause in the treaty. Actually, apart from getting an internationally recognized justification for withdrawal, an injured country could not expect much from the United Nations, even if an offender had been condemned by the Security Council. In the prevailing political circumstances, a collective punitive action against a transgressor of an arms control treaty is unthinkable.[5]

A withdrawal clause is normally not keyed specifically to violations, but to occurrence of "extraordinary events" related to the subject matter of the treaty, which have "jeopardized the supreme interests" of the party in question. Nevertheless, in the absence of a formal U.N. verdict that a violation had been committed, a unilateral decision to withdraw from a treaty (or to suspend the operation of the treaty with the defaulting state, according to general principles of international law) could be politically hazardous. To be on the safe side, the complaining state would need to possess convincing evidence of a violation. And to impress world opinion, the proof would have to be authoritatively confirmed by an impartial expert inquiry.

First steps towards separating international fact-finding from U.N. political judgment have been made in the recently signed convention on environmental warfare, the so-called ENMOD Convention.[6] The convention stipulates that consultations to clarify problems relating to the objectives of the convention and to its application may include the services of international organization (such as, for example, the World Meteorological Organization or the U.N. Environment Program) and, what is more significant, a consultative committee of experts to be convened upon request. The role of the committee will be restricted to providing expert views on issues raised, and no voting on matters of substance is to be allowed. This is not an entirely satisfactory solution, but the right to decide procedural questions relative to the organization of its work, by a majority, may enable the committee to order an inquiry.[7] And since a summary of the findings, incorporating all views and information presented to the committee during its proceedings, is to be distributed to the parties, the prevailing range of opinions on matters of substance can be made discernible without recourse to voting. The essential point is that experts will be given an opportunity to examine the particulars of each case and make their views widely known, irrespective of whether or not the case will eventually be considered by the Security Council. It would be up to the complaining country to draw its own conclusions from the information received and to decide upon further action. The new procedure is definitely an advance over previous practice and a precedent for future treaties of a similar nature.

All this does not solve the dilemma of how governments, other than those of the major powers, would acquire information to justify setting in motion the consultative and investigative machineries. With the exception of non-proliferation obligations under the Non-Proliferation Treaty and the Treaty of Tlatelolco, which are checked on a continuous basis through a system of nuclear safeguards operated internationally, means of verifying compliance have been practically a monopoly of the great powers. Because of the small disarmament value of the treaties concluded hitherto, the problem has not, as yet, figured prominently in the negotiations. But it will be impossible to ignore it in a convention prohibiting the production and stockpiling of chemical weapons or in a treaty banning underground nuclear explosions, both of which are generally considered as important measures. As a matter of fact, the need to include some standard verification procedures in these two agreements has already been recognized in principle, and some detailed proposals have been made.

Thus, two drafts of a convention dealing with chemical weapons envisage the establishment of an international organ, called either the International Verification Agency or Consultative Committee, to oversee the working of the convention. This organ would receive, analyze and evaluate periodic reports, as well as statistical and other information submitted by the parties. It would also be its duty to consult and cooperate with national authorities responsible for the implementation of the convention, observe and verify what was being destroyed or converted to peaceful uses, and conduct the necessary inquiries.[8]

A proposal concerning the cessation of nuclear-weapon explosions provides for international centers whose main function would be to collect data about seismic events, evaluate them, and distribute the results to the parties. In addition, a draft test-ban treaty envisages the services of a consultative committee to which any party may appoint a representative.[9]

Institutions to deal with the verification of specific arms control agreements could be set up either as autonomous bodies or as parts of the international agencies already in existence. (An example of the latter approach is the current use of the International Atomic Energy Agency to check the implementation of the Non-Proliferation Treaty, although its main task is to promote the peaceful uses of nuclear energy.) But there have also been suggestions for the establishment of a global agency covering all arms-control and disarmament measures.[10] The idea is not new. As early as 1933, the states negotiating a convention for the reduction and limitation of armaments at the League of Nations Disarmament Conference agreed that a permanent disarmament commission should be set up to "watch the execution of the convention."[11] The commission would receive all relevant information, including complaints about infringements, and would be entitled to request the parties to supply necessary explanations, as well as to hear or consult with any person in a position to throw light on the question examined. It would be empowered not only to investigate alleged infractions of the convention, but also to conduct periodic inspections. The powers of the commission would, furthermore, include preparations of agreements as might be necessary to ensure the implementation of the convention, preparations for a conference on subsequent stages of disarmament, and the undertaking of studies useful for the fulfillment of its duties.

More recently, the need for a disarmament agency was recognized in a joint U.S.-Soviet statement (the so-called McCloy-Zorin statement) dealing with negotiations for a general and complete disarmament.[12] One of the principles included in the statement stipulates that to "implement control over and inspection of disarmament" an international disarmament organization should be created within the framework of the United Nations. Accordingly, the proposed Soviet draft treaty on general and complete disarmament of 1962 provided that an organization of the parties to the treaty would begin operating as soon as disarmament measures were initiated.[13] The organization would receive information about the armed forces, armaments, military production and military appropriations supplied by the parties, and would have its own staff, recruited internationally, to exercise control on a temporary or permanent basis, depending on the nature of the measure being carried out. The United States envisaged the establishment of an international organization with the purpose of ensuring that all obligations were honored and observed during and after implementation of general and complete disarmament.[14] It requested that inspectors of the organization should have unrestricted access without veto to all such places as were necessary for the purpose of effective verification.

Whatever the differences about the composition or terms of reference of a possible international disarmament organization, there seems to be a consensus that comprehensive and general disarmament would require a comprehensive treatment of verification on a global scale to guard against the risks to vital security interests of states. Whether a global verification organization is necessary to deal with disparate, partial measures is a moot question.

Those who advocate overall arrangements at the present stage, that is, even before a comprehensive disarmament program has been agreed upon, argue that verification of compliance is an international responsibility; that dissemination of information about arms and disarmament must be institutionalized to increase confidence in the existing agreements and to accelerate negotiations on further agreements; and that there is a need to centralize the tasks at present performed by the depositary governments, such as the convening of review conferences to check on and possibly suggest amendments for arms control treaties.[15]

On the other hand, there does not seem to be much that an omnibus disarmament organization could do with respect to the verification of existing multilateral arms control agreements. Most of them are not likely to be violated, anyway. New multilateral treaties, such as a convention prohibiting chemical weapons or a comprehensive nuclear test ban treaty, will require specialized expert bodies applying their own rules in handling verification issues; the choice of control methods will depend on the type of activity prohibited and on the technical means available. In each case different factors will have to be taken into account to initiate and carry out an inquiry. Maximum use will probably be made of U.N.-affiliated and other authoritative international institutions dealing with related peaceful activities.

In regional agreements, the parties are likely to rely on regional rather than world-wide verification arrangements. Thus, for example, the members of the Treaty of Tlatelolco have preferred to establish their own machinery to keep Latin America free from nuclear weapons and have assigned only a subsidiary role to the International Atomic Energy Agency. The Western European Union has its own Armaments Control Agency to verify that the member states are observing the regional armaments limitations to which they agreed. Similarly, any reduction of forces in Central Euorpe that may result from the current Vienna talks will most probably be supervised only by the countries directly concerned.

In U.S.-Soviet relations, a Standing Consultative Commission has been created to consider questions of compliance, organize the exchange of information and discuss proposals for increasing the viability of the strategic arms control treaties. Apparently, the commission has been functioning quite satisfactorily and there is no indication that in future agreements the two powers would need or, indeed, would be willing to resort to a larger forum and relegate their bilateral problems to some third-party consideration.

There remains the question of the widest possible spread of knowledge about armament developments in general, irrespective of treaty limitations. This is a matter of great importance, as the scope of disarmament treaties may depend on the degree of openness among nations with regard to weapons production and deployment, arms transfers and military expenditure. However, an international organizational framework for such activities already exists within the United Nations. Recently, the U.N. Secretariat has been given a specific task to improve its facilities for the dissemination of relevant information.[16] Organizational measures are, of course, not enough to reduce secretiveness in military matters. As long as governments cling to their conservative views on national security, they will be reluctant to provide information to any intergovernmental body, be it the United Nations or other organizations, and most states will have no choice but to rely on non-governmental data collection and analysis.

In conclusion, a global verification institution seems to be a commendable long-term goal, when linked with a comprehensive program of disarmament. In the immediate future, however, each multilateral arms control treaty should provide for a special mechanism through which information about compliance with the obligations acquired by some parties, in particular, information gathered by sophisticated technical methods, would be shared by all parties.

At the same time, it is appropriate to devote attention to the strengthening of the newly created U.N. Center for Disarmament which is to perform certain auxiliary functions related to the implementation of agreements.[17] While perhaps not in a position to carry out control duties, the center could, perhaps, gradually assume the role of coordinator of operations conducted by bodies directly involved in the verification of different arms control measures. In any event, the potentialities of this new unit ought to be fully tested before the establishment of a new institution is contemplated.

Notes

1. In April, 1926, U.S. Secretary of State F.B. Kellogg instructed the American delegation participating in the work of the Preparatory Commission for the Disarmament Conference to defend the following position: "The execution of any international agreement for the limitation of armaments must depend in so far as the United States is concerned upon international good faith and respect for treaties. The United States will not tolerate the supervision of any outside body in this matter nor be subject to inspection or supervision by foreign agencies or individuals." *Foreign Relations of the United States, Diplomatic Papers (General) 1926 Volume 1*, p. 88.

It took several years for the United States to revise its view. In a May, 1933, statement at the Disarmament Conference, the U.S. delegate said: "We are heartily in sympathy with the idea that means of effective, automatic and continuous supervision should be found whereby nations will be able to rest assured that as long as they respect their obligations with regard to armaments, the corresponding obligations of their neighbors will be carried out in the same scrupulous manner." *Foreign Relations of the United States, Diplomatic Papers, (Disarmament Conference) 1933 Volume 1*, p. 156.

This is still the position of the United States and most other states.

2. The following agreements have been examined for the purpose of this paper: the Antarctic Treaty, in force since June 23, 1961; the Partial Test Ban Treaty (PTBT) in force since October 10, 1963; the Outer Space Treaty, in force since October 10, 1967; the Treaty Prohibiting Nuclear Weapons in Latin America (Treaty of Tlatelolco), in force since 1967; the Non-Proliferation Treaty (NPT) in force since March 5, 1970; the Sea-Bed Treaty, in force since May 18, 1972; the Biological Warfare Convention (BW Convention), in force since March 26, 1975; the Convention Prohibiting Environmental Modification Techniques (ENMOD Convention), signed on May 18, 1977, but not yet in force; the U.S.-Soviet Treaty Limiting Anti-Ballistic Missile Systems (SALT ABM Treaty), in force since October 3, 1972; the U.S.-Soviet Agreement Limiting Strategic Offensive Arms (SALT Interim Agreement), in force since October 3, 1972; the U.S.-Soviet Threshold Test Ban Treaty (TTBT), signed July 3, 1974, but not yet in force; and the U.S.-Soviet Peaceful Nuclear Explosions Treaty (PNET), signed on May 28, 1976, but not yet in force. A tabulation of ways in which verification has been dealt with in some of these agreements, can be found in working papers submitted by Sweden at the Conference of the Committee on Disarmament (Disarmament Conference documents CCD/287 of April 30, 1970 and CCD/398 or April 24, 1973).

3. The document on confidence-building measures and certain aspects of security and disarmament, included in the Final Act of the Conference on Security and Cooperation in Europe of August 1, 1975, provides for prior notification of major military maneuvers, but the preamble of the document says that the measure "rests upon a voluntary basis."

4. This would apply, in the first place, to China and France — two of the five permanent members of the Security Council. China has adhered only to Additional Protocol II of the Treaty of Tlatelolco, while France, in addition to that protocol, has joined no more than two of the arms control treaties considered here — the Antarctic Treaty and the Outer Space Treaty. It will be noted that the threat of a Chinese veto has made it impossible for the Security Council formally to assume the functions assigned to it by the Biological Warfare Convention and agree, through a special resolution, to receive, consider and act upon complaints about alleged breaches of the convention.

5. For a thorough discussion of the problem of sanctions under arms control agreements, see Abram Chayes, "An Inquiry Into the Workings of Arms Control Agreements," *Harvard Law Review* Vol. 85, No. 5 (March 1972).

6. For an analysis of the verification provisions of the Environmental Modification Techniques Convention see Jozef Goldblat, "The Environmental Warfare Convention: How Meaningful Is It?" *Ambio* (Journal of the Royal Swedish Academy of Sciences) Vol. 6, No. 4 (1977).

7. According to a proposal put forward by the Netherlands and Sweden during the informal meetings at the Disarmament Conference in 1976, the consultative body would be a standing organ (not a committee constituted *ad hoc*) with the right to initiate an inquiry into relevant facts. It would also be entitled to consider proposals for improving the viability of the convention, including recommendations for amendments.

8. See Conference of the Committee on Disarmament, draft conventions on the Prohibition of the Development, Production and Stockpiling of Chemical Weapons and on their Destruction, submitted by Japan (Disarmament Conference document CCD/420) and the United Kingdom (Disarmament

Conference document CCD/512) on April 30, 1974 and August 6, 1976, respectively. A detailed description of the possible structure of an international standing organ in the context of a chemical warfare convention can be found in a working paper prepared by the Netherlands (Conference of the Committee on Disarmament, Disarmament Conference document CCD/410 of July 31, 1973).

9. See Conference of the Committee on Disarmament, Working Paper on Cooperative International Measures to Monitor a CTB, submitted by Sweden on March 26, 1976 (Disarmament Conference document CCD/482) and Draft Treaty Banning Nuclear Weapon Test Explosions in all Environments, of March 1, 1977, also submitted by Sweden (Disarmament Conference document CCD/526).

10. See Conference of the Committee on Disarmament, statement by the Swedish representative at the Geneva Disarmament Conference on April 17, 1973 (Disarmament Conference document CCD/PV.601). The subject is dealt with in detail in Alva Myrdal, "The International Control of Disarmament," *Scientific American* Vol. 231, No. 4 (October 1974).

11. See League of Nations document Conf. D. 163(I) in *Series of League of Nations Publications,* IX, Disarmament, 1936, IX, 3.

12. See Joint Statement of Agreed Principles of Disarmament Negotiations of September 20, 1961 (U.N. document A/4879).

13. See Disarmament Conference document ENDC/2 of March 19, 1962.

14. See Disarmament Conference document ENDC/30 of April 18, 1962.

15. See footnote 10.

16. See U.N. General Assembly resolution 31/90 of December 14, 1976.

17. Under the Environmental Modifications Techniques Convention, the U.N. secretary general has been given the task of being the depositary of the convention, as well as the duty to convene a consultative committee of experts and conferences to review the operation of the convention. Future multilateral arms control treaties will probably follow the same pattern.

Appendix I

REPORT
OF THE PREPARATORY
COMMITTEE FOR THE SPECIAL
SESSION OF THE
GENERAL ASSEMBLY
DEVOTED TO DISARMAMENT

GENERAL ASSEMBLY
OFFICIAL RECORDS: THIRTY-SECOND SESSION
SUPPLEMENT No. 41 (A/32/41)

UNITED NATIONS
New York, 1977

I. INTRODUCTION

1.   At its thirty-first session, the General Assembly adopted resolution 31/189 B of 21 December 1976, the operative part of which reads as follows:

"The General Assembly,

"1. *Decides* to convene a special session of the General Assembly devoted to disarmament, to be held in New York in May/June 1978;

"2. *Further decides* to establish a Preparatory Committee for the Special Session of the General Assembly Devoted to Disarmament, composed of fifty-four Member States appointed by the President of the Assembly on the basis of equitable geographical distribution, with the mandate of examining all relevant questions relating to the special session, including its agenda, and of submitting to the Assembly at its thirty-second session appropriate recommendations thereon;

"3. *Invites* all Member States to communicate to the Secretary-General their views on the agenda and all other relevant questions relating to the special session of the General Assembly not later than 15 April 1977;

"4. *Requests* the Secretary-General to transmit the replies of Member States pursuant to paragraph 3 above to the Preparatory Committee and to render it all necessary assistance, including the provision of essential background information, relevant documents and summary records;

"5. *Requests* the Preparatory Committee to meet for a short organizational session of not longer than one week, before 31 March 1977, *inter alia,* to set the dates for its substantive sessions;

"6. *Decides* to include in the provisional agenda of its thirty-second session an item entitled: 'Special session of the General Assembly devoted to disarmament: report of the Preparatory Committee for the Special Session of the General Assembly Devoted to Disarmament'."

2.   In accordance with paragraph 2 of the resolution, the President of the General Assembly, after consultations with the Chairmen of the regional groups, appointed the following countries to be members of the Preparatory Committee: Algeria, Argentina, Australia, Austria, Bahamas, Bangladesh, Belgium, Benin, Brazil, Burundi, Canada, Colombia, Cuba, Cyprus, Egypt, Ethiopia, France, German Democratic Republic, Germany, Federal Republic of, Guyana, Hungary, India, Iran, Iraq, Italy, Japan, Liberia, Libyan Arab Jamahiriya, Malaysia, Mauritius, Mexico, Morocco,

Nepal, Nigeria, Norway, Pakistan, Panama, Peru, Philippines, Poland, Romania, Spain, Sri Lanka, Sudan, Sweden, Tunisia, Turkey, Union of Soviet Socialist Republics, United Kingdom of Great Britain and Northern Ireland, United States of America, Venezuela, Yugoslavia, Zaire and Zambia.

3.   In connexion with the representation of the countries of the Eastern European Group in the Preparatory Committee, the Chairman of that Group addressed a letter to the President of the General Assembly, dated 3 February 1977 (A/31/475) expressing disagreement with the allocation of six instead of eight seats to the Eastern European Group and reserving its right to raise the question of allocating additional seats in the Preparatory Committee at the thirty-second session of the General Assembly. Views to that effect and on other aspects of the question of the membership of the Committee were also expressed at the sessions of the Preparatory Committee and are reflected in the summary records (A/AC.187/SR.1-20).

4.   Pursuant to paragraph 3 of the resolution, the Secretary-General addressed a note verbale, dated 28 January 1977, to all Member States inviting them to communicate their views on the agenda and all other relevant questions relating to the special session of the General Assembly not later than 15 April 1977. Written replies from 58 States were circulated as documents (A/32/60, A/32/62; A/AC.187/2-28, 32-42 and Corr.1, 44-50, 52, 53, 57-59, 61, 63-66 and 83).

II. ORGANIZATION OF THE WORK OF THE COMMITTEE

5.   Pursuant to paragraph 5 of General Assembly resolution 31/189 B, the Committee met at United Nations Headquarters in an organizational session from 28 to 30 March, and in substantive sessions from 9 to 20 May and from 31 August to 9 September 1977. During these three sessions the Committee held 20 meetings. The Committee also held seven informal meetings during the period from 22 to 30 August. In addition, members of the Committee held intensive consultations during and in between sessions of the Committee. The 1st meeting of the Committee, held on 28 March, was opened by the Secretary-General, who made a statement (CA/AC.187/62).

6.   The Committee elected the following officers:

Chairman:	H.E. Mr. Carlos Ortiz de Rozas	(Argentina)
Vice-Chairmen:	H.E. Mr. Isao Abe	(Japan)
	H.E. Mr. Leslie O. Harriman	(Nigeria)
	H.E. Mr. Ralph L. Harry, C.B.E.	(Australia)
	H.E. Mr. Fereydoun Hoveyda	(Iran)

H.E. Mr. Henryk Jaroszek	(Poland)
H.E. Mr. Livingston B. Johnson	(Bahamas)
H.E. Mr. Jaksa Petrić	(Yugoslavia)
H.E. Mr. Oscar Vaernø	(Norway)
Rapporteur: Mr. Saad Alfarargi	(Egypt)

7.   At the same meeting, the Committee agreed to be governed by the relevant parts of the rules of procedure of the General Assembly in taking decisions. Notwithstanding that fact, it had been generally agreed during consultations that every effort should be made to ensure that, in so far as possible, decisions on matters of substance were adopted by consensus. Should efforts to secure a consensus fail, decisions could then be adopted in accordance with the provisions of the rules of procedure of the General Assembly.

8.   Also at the same meeting, the Committee agreed that non-member States of the Committee could participate in plenary meetings without the right to vote. The following countries attended the Committee's meetings: Bulgaria, Chile, Czechoslovakia, Denmark, Finland, Greece, Honduras, Ireland, Israel, Lebanon, Mongolia, Netherlands, New Zealand, Portugal and Syrian Arab Republic. The representative of the Holy See also attended the meetings.

9.   At its 4th meeting, on 9 May, the Committee agreed to a recommendation made by its bureau that representatives of non-governmental organizations could be present at meetings of the Preparatory Committee and that, in order to facilitate dissemination of information on contributions of non-governmental organizations, the Secretariat would provide lists, for general circulation, of the communications received from the organizations and institutions known to be conducting research in the field of disarmament. The lists would indicate where the communications and any annexed documentation would be available to delegations.[1]

10.   At its sixth meeting, on 10 May, the Committee decided that specialized agencies concerned with disarmament and the International Atomic Energy Agency (IAEA) should be invited to take part in the work of the Committee with observer status. Representatives of the United Nations Educational, Scientific and Cultural Organization (UNESCO) and the International Atomic Energy Agency (IAEA) have attended the meetings of the Committee.

---

[1]Lists of communications received from non-governmental organizations and research institutions are contained in documents A/AC.187/INF.2-4.

11.   At its 2nd meeting, on 28 March, the Committee requested the Secretariat to prepare background papers on the following subjects:

(a) Disarmament resolutions adopted by the General Assembly from 1946 to 1976 (A/AC.187/29 and Corr. 1);

(b) Existing principles and proposals for the conduct of disarmament negotiations (A/AC.187/30 and Corr. 1);

(c) Existing structures and machinery for disarmament negotiations (A/AC.187/31).

12.   At its 6th meeting, on 11 May, the Committee requested the Secretariat to prepare a document classifying, under various headings, the replies received from Governments pursuant to paragraph 3 of resolution 31/189 B. At its 7th meeting, on 12 May, the Committee approved a list of headings to be used by the Secretariat in fulfilling the task assigned to it (A/AC.187/51 and Corr. 1 and 2 and Add.1). At the same meeting, the Committee requested that the opinions expressed by delegations during its general debate be included in a subsequent document (A/AC.187/76).

13.   At its 14th meeting, on 20 May, the Committee requested the Secretariat to prepare the following working papers:

(a) A brief synopsis of negotiations on disarmament and arms limitation, including their results, carried out since 1945 within the framework of the United Nations, on a regional basis or bilaterally, with an indication, when appropriate, of the procedures followed in each case to keep the Organization informed (A/AC.187/67);

(b) A comparative study of the scope originally proposed or aimed at in draft multilateral disarmament treaties of a universal character concluded under United Nations auspices and the scope finally fixed in those treaties, including the contemplated measures for expanding that scope (A/AC.187/68);

(c) A comprehensive study of official proposals or declarations made and decisions taken by the General Assembly on the procedure of unilateral or negotiated moratoria as a provisional measure for the prohibition of nuclear-weapon tests, as well as their application by any State (A/AC.187/69);

(d) A synthesis of the arguments adduced for and against each of the four proposals for the creation of nuclear-weapon-free zones that have been included in the General Assembly's agenda (Africa, South Asia, the Middle East and the South

Pacific) and for and against the proposal for the establishment of a zone of peace in the Indian Ocean, including a subject index and a country index (A/AC.187/70);

(e) A comparative study of the origin, development and present status of various alternatives proposed for the prohibition of the use of nuclear weapons (A/AC.187/71);

(f) An analytical summary of United Nations studies describing the effects of the possible use of nuclear weapons, chemical weapons, bacteriological (biological) weapons and napalm and other incendiary weapons, as well as those dealing with the reduction of military budgets, the economic and social consequences of the arms race and disarmament and with the relationship between development and disarmament (A/AC.187/72);

(g) A comparative study of global military expenditures and development assistance since 1945 as stated in official and unofficial sources (A/AC.187/73);

(h) A descriptive report on the human and material resources available to the United Nations Secretariat for its work on disarmament and on the organization of that work (A/AC.187/74);

(i) A list of disarmament and related proposals officially submitted to the United Nations describing the proposal, the date and country of submission and the follow-up (A/AC.187/75).

14.   The proceedings of the meetings, including the views expressed by delegations, are contained in the summary records (A/AC.187/SR.1 to 20).

III. DOCUMENTS SUBMITTED BY MEMBER STATES

15.   In the course of the Committee's work, the following documents dealing with substantive questions were submitted:

(a) Working paper entitled "Some preliminary ideas concerning preparations for the special session of the General Assembly devoted to disarmament", submitted by Sri Lanka on behalf of the Co-ordinating Bureau of the Non-Aligned Countries (A/AC.187/55);

(b) Working paper entitled "Some fundamental principles and norms possible for inclusion in the 'Declaration on Disarmament' envisaged in the draft agenda of the special session of the General Assembly devoted to disarmament, approved by the Preparatory Committee on 18 May 1977", submitted by Mexico (A/AC.187/56);

(c) Working paper containing elements to be included in the declaration on disarmament, submitted by Mauritius (A/AC.187/60, annex);

(d) Working paper entitled "Declaration on disarmament", submitted by Romania (A/AC.187/77);

(e) Working paper entitled "Programme of measures and action", submitted by Romania (A/AC.187/78);

(f) Working paper entitled "Negotiating machinery for disarmament problems", submitted by Romania (A/AC.187/79);

(g) Working paper entitled "Disarmament and development: proposal for a United Nations study", submitted by Denmark, Finland, Norway and Sweden (A/AC.187/80);

(h) Working paper entitled "Basic provisions of the declaration on disarmament", submitted by Bulgaria, Czechoslovakia, the German Democratic Republic, Hungary, Mongolia, Poland and the Union of Soviet Socialist Republics (A/AC.187/81);

(i) Working paper entitled "Basic provisions of the programme of action on disarmament", submitted by Bulgaria, Czechoslovakia, the German Democratic Republic, Hungary, Mongolia, Poland and the Union of Soviet Socialist Republics (A/AC.187/82).

IV. RECOMMENDATIONS OF THE PREPARATORY COMMITTEE

16. At its 15th to 18th meetings, the Committee decided by consensus to submit the recommendations set forth in paragraphs 17 to 25 below to the General Assembly at its thirty-second session with regard to the organization of the work of the special session of the General Assembly devoted to disarmament and the future work of the Preparatory Committee.

A. *Organization of the work of the special session*

1. *Provisional agenda*

17. The Committee recommends the following provisional agenda for the special session:

1. Opening of the session in accordance with rule 30 of the rules of procedure of the General Assembly.

2. Minute of silent prayer or meditation.

3. Credentials of representatives to the eighth special session of the General Assembly:

(a) Appointment of the members of the Credentials Committee;

(b) Report of the Credentials Committee.

4. Election of the President of the General Assembly.

5. Organization of the session.

6. Report of the Preparatory Committee for the Special Session of the General Assembly Devoted to Disarmament.

7. Adoption of the agenda.

8. General debate.

9. Review and appraisal of the present international situation in the light of the pressing need to achieve substantial progress in the field of disarmament, the continuation of the arms race and the close interrelationship between disarmament, international peace and security and economic development.

10. Adoption of a declaration on disarmament.

11. Adoption of a programme of action on disarmament.

12. Review of the role of the United Nations in disarmament and of the international machinery for negotiations on disarmament, including, in particular, the question of convening a world disarmament conference.

18.   In connexion with the provisional agenda, the Preparatory Committee recommends that the General Assembly, at its thirty-second session, should request the Conference of the Committee on Disarmament to submit to it at its special session a special report on the state of the various questions under consideration by the Conference. The Preparatory Committee also recommends that the General Assembly, at its thirty-second session, should request the *Ad Hoc* Committee on the World Disarmament Conference to submit a special report to the special session on the state of its work and deliberations. These special reports would be submitted to the special session with the report of the Preparatory Committee, as part of the documentation prepared for the special session.

2. Date and duration

19.   The special session should be held between 23 May and 28 June 1978 in New York in the General Assembly Hall.

20.   In light of the programme of alterations scheduled to take place at the Headquarters building in New York in 1978 and 1979, as decided by the General Assembly in resolution 31/195, the Committee recommends that, at its thirty-second session, the Assembly should take a decision, by 15 October

1977, to reverse the phases of the construction work at Headquarters and thereby make the General Assembly Hall available for the special session in 1978.

3. *President*

21.   The Committee considers that, following the practice of previous special sessions, the General Assembly may wish to elect the President of the thirty-second session as the President of the special session.

4. *Vice-Presidents*

22.   Vice-Presidents of the special session should be the same as at the thirty-second regular session of the General Assembly, on the understanding that regional groups may make substitutions of Vice-Presidents allocated to each group.

5. *Main Committees*

23.   The special session should establish a committee of the whole, with as many open-ended groups or subsidiary organs as may be necessary. The Chairman of the committee of the whole should be elected by the Assembly at its special session.

6. *Credentials Committee*

24.   The Credentials Committee of the special session should be the same as that of the thirty-second regular session of the General Assembly.

7. *General Committee*

25.   The General Committee of the special session should consist of the President of the special session of the General Assembly, the 17 Vice-Presidents and the Chairmen of the seven Main Committees of the thirty-second session of the General Assembly, on the understanding that they may be substituted by members of their delegations or members of delegations of States belonging to the same regional group, the Chairman of the committee of the whole of the special session and the Chairman of the Preparatory Committee for the Special Session of the General Assembly Devoted to Disarmament.

8. *Rules of procedure*

26.   The rules of procedure of the General Assembly should apply in the special session without amendments, on the understanding that, regarding the adoption of decisions by the Assembly at the special session, every effort should be made to ensure that, in so far as possible, decisions on matters of substance will be adopted by consensus.

9. *Level of representation*

27.   It would be desirable that Member States be represented at the special session at the highest possible level.

10. *Public information activities*

28.   The Committee recommends adoption of the programme of public information activities submitted by the Secretariat (A/AC.187/83), on the understanding that, in so far as possible, such activities should be carried out within the regular budget of the Office of Public Information.

11. *Role of non-governmental organizations*

29.   The Committee recommends that non-governmental organizations concerned with disarmament should be accorded the same facilities at the special session as those which they have received at the Preparatory Committee.

B. *Organization of the future work of the Preparatory Committee for the Special Session of the General Assembly Devoted to Disarmament*

30.   The Preparatory Committee should hold two additional sessions in 1978 before the convening of the special session: one from 24 January to 24 February and the other from 10 to 21 April 1978.

31.   In connexion with the fourth session of the Committee, to be held between 24 January and 24 February 1978, it was decided that the Committee will become a working group open to those members of the Committee wishing to participate in it, leaving open the possibility of establishing one or more subgroups, as necessary. A decision as to whether the working group will meet formally or informally will be taken by the working group itself.

C. *Other recommendations*

32.   In connexion with the proposal submitted by Denmark, Finland, Norway and Sweden contained in the working paper entitled "Disarmament and development: proposal for a United Nations study" (A/AC.1/187/80), the Committee recommends that the General Assembly should initiate the proposed study, the terms of reference and other aspects of the study to be determined by the Assembly itself, and further recommends that decisions in that respect should be taken at the special session.

V. PRINCIPAL DOCUMENTS OF THE SPECIAL SESSION

33.   The Committee reached consensus, in principle, that, without excluding other possibilities, the main elements of the principal document or documents of the special session should be:

(a) Introduction or preamble;

(b) Declaration on disarmament;

(c) Programme of action;

(d) Machinery for disarmament negotiations.

It was noted that there was a trend in the Committee in favour of one final document, but it was agreed that this question should be decided at a later stage.

Appendix II

Treaty on the Non-Proliferation of Nuclear Weapons

**Signed at London, Moscow, and Washington July 1, 1968.
Entered into force March 5, 1970.**

The States concluding this Treaty, hereinafter referred to as the "Parties to the Treaty,"

Considering the devastation that would be visited upon all mankind by a nuclear war and the consequent need to make every effort to avert the danger of such a war and to take measures to safeguard the security of peoples,

Believing that the proliferation of nuclear weapons would seriously enhance the danger of nuclear war,

In conformity with resolutions of the United Nations General Assembly calling for the conclusion of an agreement on the prevention of wider dissemination of nuclear weapons,

Undertaking to cooperate in facilitating the application of International Atomic Energy Agency safeguards on peaceful nuclear activities,

Expressing their support for research, development and other efforts to further the application, within the framework of the International Atomic Energy Agency safeguards system, of the principle of safeguarding effectively the flow of source and special fissionable materials by use of instruments and other techniques at certain strategic points,

Affirming the principle that the benefits of peaceful applications of nuclear technology, including any technological byproducts which may be derived by nuclear-weapon States from the development of nuclear explosive devices, should be available for peaceful purposes to all Parties to the Treaty, whether nuclear-weapon or non-nuclear-weapon States,

Convinced that, in furtherance of this principle, all Parties to the Treaty are entitled to participate in the fullest possible exchange of scientific information for, and to contribute alone or in cooperation with other States to, the further development of the applications of atomic energy for peaceful purposes,

Declaring their intention to achieve at the earliest possible date the cessation of the nuclear arms race and to undertake effective measures in the direction of nuclear disarmament,

Urging the cooperation of all States in the attainment of this objective,

Recalling the determination expressed by the Parties to the 1963 Treaty banning nuclear weapon tests in the atmosphere in outer space and under water in its Preamble to seek to achieve the discontinuance of all test explosions of nuclear weapons for all time and to continue negotiations to this end,

Desiring to further the easing of international tension and the strengthening of trust between States in order to facilitate the cessation of the manufacture of nuclear weapons, the liquidation of all their existing stockpiles, and the elimination from national arsenals of nuclear weapons and the means of their delivery pursuant to a treaty on general and complete disarmament under strict and effective international control,

Recalling that, in accordance with the Charter of the United Nations, States must refrain in their international relations from the threat or use of force against the territorial integrity or political independence of any State, or in any other manner inconsistent with the Purposes of the United Nations, and that the establishment and maintenance of international peace and security are to be promoted with the least diversion for armaments of the world's human and economic resources,

Have agreed as follows:

ARTICLE I

Each nuclear-weapon State Party to the Treaty undertakes not to transfer to any recipient whatsoever nuclear weapons or other nuclear explosive devices or control over such weapons or explosive devices directly, or indirectly; and not in any way to assist, encourage, or induce any non-nuclear-weapon State to manufacture or otherwise acquire nuclear weapons or other nuclear explosive devices or control over such weapons or explosive devices.

ARTICLE II

Each non-nuclear-weapon State Party to the Treaty undertakes not to receive the transfer from any transferor whatsoever of nuclear weapons or other nuclear explosive devices or of control over such weapons or explosive devices directly, or indirectly; not to manufacture or otherwise acquire nuclear weapons or other nuclear explosive devices; and not to seek or receive any assistance in the manufacture of nuclear weapons or other nuclear explosive devices.

ARTICLE III

1. Each non-nuclear-weapon State Party to the Treaty

undertakes to accept safeguards, as set forth in an agreement to be negotiated and concluded with the International Atomic Energy Agency in accordance with the Statute of the International Atomic Energy Agency and the Agency's safeguards system, for the exclusive purpose of verification of the fulfillment of its obligations assumed under this Treaty with a view to preventing diversion of nuclear energy from peaceful uses to nuclear weapons or other nuclear explosive devices. Procedures for the safeguards required by this article shall be followed with respect to source or special fissionable material whether it is being produced, processed or used in any principal nuclear facility or is outside any such facility. The safeguards required by this article shall be applied on all source or special fissionable material in all peaceful nuclear activities within the territory of such State, under its jurisdiction, or carried out under its control anywhere.

2. Each State Party to the Treaty undertakes not to provide: (a) source or special fissionable material, or (b) equipment or material especially designed or prepared for the processing, use or production of special fissionable material, to any non-nuclear-weapon State for peaceful purposes, unless the source or special fissionable material shall be subject to the safeguards required by this article.

3. The safeguards required by this article shall be implemented in a manner designed to comply with article IV of this Treaty, and to avoid hampering the economic or technological development of the Parties or international cooperation in the field of peaceful nuclear activities, including the international exchange of nuclear material and equipment for the processing, use or production of nuclear material for peaceful purposes in accordance with the provisions of this article and the principle of safeguarding set forth in the Preamble of the Treaty.

4. Non-nuclear-weapon States Party to the Treaty shall conclude agreements with the International Atomic Energy Agency to meet the requirements of this article either individually or together with other States in accordance with the Statute of the International Atomic Energy Agency. Negotiation of such agreements shall commence within 180 days from the original entry into force of this Treaty. For States depositing their instruments of ratification or accession after the 180-day period, negotiation of such agreements shall commence not later than the date of such deposit. Such agreements shall enter into force not later than eighteen months after the date of initiation of negotiations.

ARTICLE IV

1. Nothing in this Treaty shall be interpreted as affecting the inalienable right of all the Parties to the Treaty to develop research, production and use of nuclear energy for peaceful purposes without discrimination and in conformity with articles I and II of this Treaty.

2. All the Parties to the Treaty undertake to facilitate, and have the right to participate in, the fullest possible exchange of equipment, materials and scientific and technological information for the peaceful uses of nuclear energy. Parties to the Treaty in a position to do so shall also cooperate in contributing alone or together with other States or international organizations to the further development of the applications of nuclear energy for peaceful purposes, especially in the territories of non-nuclear-weapon States Party to the Treaty, with due consideration for the needs of the developing areas of the world.

ARTICLE V

Each Party to the Treaty undertakes to take appropriate measures to ensure that, in accordance with this Treaty, under appropriate international observation and through appropriate international procedures, potential benefits from any peaceful applications of nuclear explosions will be made available to non-nuclear-weapon States Party to the Treaty on a non-discriminatory basis and that the charge to such Parties for the explosive devices used will be as low as possible and exclude any charge for research and development. Non-nuclear-weapon States Party to the Treaty shall be able to obtain such benefits, pursuant to a special international agreement or agreements, through an appropriate international body with adequate representation of non-nuclear-weapon States. Negotiations on this subject shall commence as soon as possible after the Treaty enters into force. Non-nuclear-weapon States Party to the Treaty so desiring may also obtain such benefits pursuant to bilateral agreements.

ARTICLE VI

Each of the Parties to the Treaty undertakes to pursue negotiations in good faith on effective measures relating to cessation of the nuclear arms race at an early date and to nuclear disarmament, and on a treaty on general and complete disarmament under strict and effective international control.

ARTICLE VII

Nothing in this Treaty affects the right of any group of

States to conclude regional treaties in order to assure the total absence of nuclear weapons in their respective territories.

ARTICLE VIII

1. Any Party to the Treaty may propose amendments to this Treaty. The text of any proposed amendment shall be submitted to the Depositary Governments which shall circulate it to all Parties to the Treaty. Thereupon, if requested to do so by one-third or more of the Parties to the Treaty, the Depositary Governments shall convene a conference, to which they shall invite all the Parties to the Treaty, to consider such an amendment.

2. Any amendment to this Treaty must be approved by a majority of the votes of all the Parties to the Treaty, including the votes of all nuclear-weapon States Party to the Treaty and all the other Parties which, on the date the amendment is circulated, are members of the Board of Governors of the International Atomic Energy Agency. The amendment shall enter into force for each Party that deposits its instrument of ratification of the amendment upon the deposit of such instruments of ratification by a majority of all the Parties, including the instruments of ratification of all nuclear-weapon States Party to the Treaty and all other Parties which, on the date the amendment is circulated, are members of the Board of Governors of the International Atomic Energy Agency. Thereafter, it shall enter into force for any other Party upon the deposit of its instrument of ratification of the amendment.

3. Five years after the entry into force of this Treaty, a conference of Parties to the Treaty shall be held in Geneva, Switzerland, in order to review the operation of this Treaty with a view to assuring that the purposes of the Preamble and the provisions of the Treaty are being realized. At intervals of five years thereafter, a majority of the Parties to the Treaty may obtain, by submitting a proposal to this effect to the Depositary Governments, the convening of further conferences with the same objective of reviewing the operation of the Treaty.

ARTICLE IX

1. This Treaty shall be open to all States for signature. Any State which does not sign the Treaty before its entry into force in accordance with paragraph 3 of this article may accede to it at any time.

2. This Treaty shall be subject to ratification by signatory States. Instruments of ratification and instruments of accession shall be deposited with the Governments of the United States of America, the United Kingdom of Great Britain and

Northern Ireland and the Union of Soviet Socialist Republics, which are hereby designated the Depositary Governments.

3. This Treaty shall enter into force after its ratification by the States, the Governments of which are designated Depositaries of the Treaty, and forty other States signatory to this Treaty and the deposit of their instruments of ratification. For the purposes of this Treaty, a nuclear-weapon State is one which has manufactured and exploded a nuclear weapon or other nuclear explosive device prior to January 1, 1967.

4. For States whose instruments of ratification or accession are deposited subsequent to the entry into force of this Treaty, it shall enter into force on the date of the deposit of their instruments of ratification or accession.

5. The Depositary Governments shall promptly inform all signatory and acceding States of the date of each signature, the date of deposit of each instrument of ratification or of accession, the date of the entry into force of this Treaty, and the date of receipt of any requests for convening a conference or other notices.

6. This Treaty shall be registered by the Depositary Governments pursuant to article 102 of the Charter of the United Nations.

ARTICLE X

1. Each Party shall in exercising its national sovereignty have the right to withdraw from the Treaty if it decides that extraordinary events, related to the subject matter of this Treaty, have jeopardized the supreme interests of its country. It shall give notice of such withdrawal to all other Parties to the Treaty and the United Nations Security Council three months in advance. Such notice shall include a statement of the extraordinary events it regards as having jeopardized its supreme interests.

2. Twenty-five years after the entry into force of the Treaty, a conference shall be convened to decide whether the Treaty shall continue in force indefinitely, or shall be extended for an additional fixed period or periods. This decision shall be taken by a majority of the Parties to the Treaty.

ARTICLE XI

This Treaty, the English, Russian, French, Spanish and Chinese texts of which are equally authentic, shall be deposited in the archives of the Depositary Governments. Duly certified copies of this Treaty shall be transmitted by the Depositary Governments to the Governments of the signatory and acceding States.

Status of Non-Proliferation Treaty

A. Parties

Afganistan
Australia
Austria
Bahamas
Belgium
Benin
Bolivia
Botswana
Bulgaria
Burundi
Cambodia
Cameroon
Canada
Central African
  Empire
Chad
Costa Rica
Cyprus
Czechoslovakia
Denmark
Dominican
  Republic
Ecuador
El Salvador
Ethiopia
Fiji
Finland
Gabon
Gambia
Germany (East)
Germany (West)
Ghana
Greece
Grenada
Guatemala
Haiti

Holy See
Honduras
Hungary
Iceland
Iran
Iraq
Ireland
Italy
Ivory Coast
Jamaica
Japan
Jordan
Kenya
Korea
Laos
Lebanon
Lesotho
Liberia
Libya
Luxembourg
Madagascar
Malaysia
Maldive Islands
Mali
Malta
Mauritius
Mexico
Mongolia
Morocco
Nepal
Netherlands
New Zealand
Nicaragua
Nigeria
Norway
Panama

Paraguay
Peru
Philippines
Poland
Romania
Rwanda
San Marino
Senegal
Sierra Leone
Singapore
Somalia
Sudan
Surinam
Swaziland
Sweden
Switzerland
Syrian Arab
  Republic
Taiwan
Thailand
Togo
Tonga
Tunisia
Union of Soviet
  Socialist
  Republics*
United Kingdom*
United States
  of America*
Upper Volta
Uruguay
Venezuela
Vietnam
Western Samoa
Yugoslavia
Zaire

---

*Nuclear weapon state

B. Signatories

(have signed the Treaty, but have not completed the process of ratification)

Barbados	Kuwait	Turkey
Colombia	Sri Lanka	Yemen Arab
Egypt	Trinidad &	Republic (Sana)
Indonesia	Tobago	Yemen (Aden)

C. Non-Signatories

(have neither signed nor ratified the Treaty)

Albania	France*	Pakistan
Algeria	Guinea	Portugal
Argentina	Guinea-Bissau	Qatar
Bahrain	Guyana	Saudi Arabia
Bangladesh	India†	South Africa
Brazil	Israel	Spain
Burma	Korea (North)	Tanzania
Chile	Malawi	Uganda
China*	Mauritania	United Arab
Congo	Nauru	Emirates
Cuba	Niger	Zambia
	Oman	

---

*Nuclear weapon state.
†India has detonated a "peaceful nuclear device."

Appendix III

President Carter's Message to the U.S. Congress April 27, 1977

To the Congress of the United States:

The need to halt nuclear proliferation is one of mankind's most pressing challenges. Members of my Administration are now engaged in international discussions to find ways of controlling the spread of nuclear explosive capability without depriving any nation of the means to satisfy its energy needs. The domestic nuclear policies which I have already put forward will place our nation in a leadership position, setting a positive example for other nuclear suppliers as well as demonstrating the strength of our concern here at home for the hazards of a plutonium economy. Today I am submitting to the Congress a bill which would establish for the United States a strong and effective non-proliferation policy.

This bill relies heavily upon work which the Congress has already done, and I commend the Congress for these valuable initiatives. I look forward to working with the Congress to establish a strong, responsible legislative framework from which we can continue strengthened efforts to halt the spread of nuclear weapons.

Among our shared goals are: an increase in the effectiveness of international safeguards and controls on peaceful nuclear activities to prevent further proliferation of nuclear explosive devices, the establishment of common international sanctions to prevent such proliferation, an effort to encourage nations which have not ratified the Non-Proliferation Treaty to do so at the earliest possible date, and adoption of programs to enhance the reliability of the United States as a supplier of nuclear fuel.

This bill differs from pending proposals, however, in several respects:

1. It defines the immediate nuclear export conditions which we can reasonably ask other nations to meet while we negotiate stricter arrangements. The proposals currently before Congress would impose criteria that could force an immediate moratorium on our nuclear exports, adversely affecting certain allies

whose cooperation is needed if we are to achieve our ultimate objective of non-proliferation.

2. It defines additional nuclear export conditions which will be required in new agreements for civil nuclear cooperation. In particular, we will require as a continuing condition of U.S. supply that recipients have all their nuclear activities under IAEA safeguards. I view this as an interim measure and shall make it clear to all potential recipients and to other nuclear suppliers that our first preference, and continuing objective, is universal adherence to the Non-Proliferation Treaty.

3. For the near future, it attempts to tighten the conditions for U.S. nuclear cooperation through renegotiation of existing agreements to meet the same standards as those we will require in new agreements. I believe that this approach will better meet our non-proliferation objectives than will the unilateral imposition of new export licensing conditions.

4. It increases the flexibility we need to deal with an extremely complex subject. For example, instead of requiring countries that want our nuclear exports to foreswear fuel enrichment and reprocessing for all time, it allows us to draft new agreements using incentives to encourage countries not to acquire such facilities. It also permits me to grant exceptions when doing so would further our basic aim of non-proliferation. All new cooperation agreements would, of course, be subject to Congressional review.

This bill is intended to reassure other nations that the United States will be a reliable supplier of nuclear fuel and equipment for those who genuinely share our desire for non-proliferation. It will insure that when all statutory standards have been met, export licenses will be issued—or, if the judgment of the Executive Branch and the independent Nuclear Regulatory Commission should differ, that a workable mechanism exists for resolving the dispute.

Since I intend personally to oversee Executive Branch actions affecting non-proliferation, I do not think a substantial reorganization of the responsibility for nuclear exports within the Executive Branch is necessary. This conclusion is shared by the Nuclear Regulatory Commission.

The need for prompt action is great. Until domestic legislation is enacted, other countries will be reluctant to renegotiate their agreements with us, because they will fear that new legislation might suddenly change the terms of cooperation. If the incentives we offer them to renegotiate with us are not attractive enough, the United States could lose important existing safeguards and controls. And if our policy is too weak, we could find ourselves powerless to restrain a deadly world-wide expansion of nuclear explosive capability. I believe the legislation now submitted to you strikes the necessary balance.

JIMMY CARTER
The White House, *April 27, 1977.*

Appendix IV

TREATY FOR THE PROHIBITION OF NUCLEAR WEAPONS IN LATIN AMERICA
(Treaty of Tlatelolco)

Preamble

In the name of their peoples and faithfully interpreting their desires and aspirations, the Governments of the States which sign the Treaty for the Prohibition of Nuclear Weapons in Latin America,

Desiring to contribute, so far as lies in their power, towards ending the armaments race, especially in the field of nuclear weapons, and towards strengthening a world at peace, based on the sovereign equality of States, mutual respect and good neighbourliness,

Recalling that the United Nations General Assembly, in its Resolution 808 (IX), adopted unanimously as one of the three points of a coordinated programme of disarmament "the total prohibition of the use and manufacture of nuclear weapons and weapons of mass destruction of every type",

Recalling that militarily denuclearized zones are not an end in themselves but rather a means for achieving general and complete disarmament at a later stage,

Recalling United Nations General Assembly Resolution 1911 (XVIII), which established that the measures that should be agreed upon for the denuclearization of Latin America should be taken "in the light of the principles of the Charter of the United Nations and of regional agreements",

Recalling United Nations General Assembly Resolution 2028 (XX), which established the principle of an acceptable balance of mutual responsibilities and duties for the nuclear and non-nuclear powers, and

Recalling that the Charter of the Organization of American States proclaims that it is an essential purpose of the Organization to strengthen the peace and security of the hemisphere,

Convinced:

That the incalculable destructive power of nuclear weapons has made it imperative that the legal prohibition of war should be strictly observed in practice if the survival of civilization and of mankind itself is to be assured,

That nuclear weapons, whose terrible effects are suffered, indiscriminately and inexorably, by military forces and civilian population alike, constitute, through the persistence of the radio-activity they release, an attack on the integrity of the human species and ultimately may even render the whole earth uninhabitable,

That general and complete disarmament under effective international control is a vital matter which all the peoples of the world equally demand,

That the proliferation of nuclear weapons, which seems inevitable unless States, in the exercise of their sovereign rights, impose restrictions on themselves in order to prevent it, would make any agreement on disarmament enormously difficult and would increase the danger of the outbreak of a nuclear conflagration,

That the establishment of militarily denuclearized zones is closely linked with the maintenance of peace and security in the respective regions,

That the military denuclearization of vast geographical zones, adopted by the sovereign decision of the States comprised therein, will exercise a beneficial influence on other regions where similar conditions exist,

That the privileged situation of the signatory States, whose territories are wholly free from nuclear weapons, imposes upon them the inescapable duty of preserving that situation both in their own interests and for the good of mankind,

That the existence of nuclear weapons in any country of Latin America would make it a target for possible nuclear attacks and would inevitably set off, throughout the region, a ruinous race in nuclear weapons which would involve the unjustifiable diversion, for warlike purposes, of the limited resources required for economic and social development,

That the foregoing reasons, together with the traditional peace-loving outlook of Latin America, give rise to an inescapable necessity that nuclear energy should be used in that region exclusively for peaceful purposes, and that the Latin American countries should use their right to the greatest and most equitable possible access to this new source of energy in order to expedite the economic and social development of their peoples,

Convinced finally:

That the military denuclearization of Latin America—being understood to mean the undertaking entered into internationally in this Treaty to keep their territories forever free from nuclear weapons—will constitute a measure which will spare their peoples from the squandering of their limited resources on nuclear armaments and will protect them against possible nuclear attacks on their territories, and will also constitute a significant contribution towards preventing the proliferation of nuclear weapons and a powerful factor for general and complete disarmament, and

That Latin America, faithful to its tradition of universality, must not only endeavour to banish from its homelands the scourge of a nuclear war, but must also strive to promote the well-being and advancement of its peoples, at the same time cooperating in the fulfillment of the ideals of mankind, that is to say, in the consolidation of a permanent peace based on equal rights, economic fairness and social justice for all, in accordance with the principles and purposes set forth in the Charter of the United Nations and in the Charter of the Organization of American States,

Have agreed as follows:

Obligations

Article I

1.   The Contracting Parties hereby undertake to use exclusively for peaceful purposes the nuclear material and facilities which are under their jurisdiction, and to prohibit and prevent in their respective territories:

(a) The testing, use, manufacture, production or acquisition by any means whatsoever of any nuclear weapons, by the Parties themselves, directly or indirectly, on behalf of anyone else or in any other way, and

(b) The receipt, storage, installation, deployment and any form of possession of any nuclear weapons, directly or indirectly, by the Parties themselves, by anyone on their behalf or in any other way.

2.   The Contracting Parties also undertake to refrain from engaging in, encouraging or authorizing, directly or indirectly, or in any way participating in the testing, use, manufacture, production, possession or control of any nuclear weapon.

Definition of the Contracting Parties
Article 2

For the purposes of this Treaty, the Contracting Parties are those for whom the Treaty is in force.

Definition of territory
Article 3

For the purposes of this Treaty, the term "territory" shall include the territorial sea, air space and any other space over which the State exercises sovereignty in accordance with its own legislation.

Zone of application
Article 4

1.   The zone of application of this Treaty is the whole of the territories for which the Treaty is in force.

2.   Upon fulfillment of the requirements of article 28, paragraph 1, the zone of application of this Treaty shall also be that which is situated in the western hemisphere within the following limits (except the continental part of the territory of the United States of America and its territorial waters): starting at a point located at 35° north latitude, 75° west longitude; from this point directly southward to a point at 30° north latitude, 75° west longitude; from there, directly eastward to a point at 30° north latitude, 50° west longitude; from there, along a loxodromic line to a point at 5° north latitude, 20° west longitude; from there, directly southward to a point at 60° south latitude, 20° west longitude; from there, directly westward to a point at 60° south latitude, 115° west longitude; from there, directly northward to a point at 0 latitude, 115° west longitude; from there, along a loxodromic line to a point at 35° north latitude, 150° west longitude; from there, directly eastward to a point at 35° north latitude, 75° west longitude.

Definition of nuclear weapons
Article 5

For the purposes of this Treaty, a nuclear weapon is any device which is capable of releasing nuclear energy in an uncontrolled manner and which has a group of characteristics that are appropriate for use for warlike purposes. An instrument that may be used for the transport or propulsion of the device is not included in this definition if it is separable from the device and not an indivisible part thereof.

Meeting of signatories

Article 6

At the request of any of the signatory States or if the Agency established by article 7 should so decide, a meeting of all the signatories may be convoked to consider in common questions which may affect the very essence of this instrument, including possible amendments to it. In either case, the meeting will be convoked by the General Secretary.

Organization

Article 7

1.   In order to ensure compliance with the obligations of this Treaty, the Contracting Parties hereby establish an international organization to be known as the "Agency for the Prohibition of Nuclear Weapons in Latin America", hereinafter referred to as "the Agency". Only the Contracting Parties shall be affected by its decisions.

2.   The Agency shall be responsible for the holding of periodic or extraordinary consultations among Member States on matters relating to the purposes, measures and procedures set forth in this Treaty and to the supervision of compliance with the obligations arising therefrom.

3.   The Contracting Parties agree to extend to the Agency full and prompt co-operation in accordance with the provisions of this Treaty, of any agreements they may conclude with the Agency and of any agreements the Agency may conclude with any other international organization or body.

4.   The headquarters of the Agency shall be in Mexico City.

Organs

Article 8

1.   There are hereby established as principal organs of the Agency a General Conference, a Council and a Secretariat.

2.   Such subsidiary organs as are considered necessary by the General Conference may be established within the purview of this Treaty.

The General Conference

Article 9

1.   The General Conference, the supreme organ of the Agency, shall be composed of all the Contracting Parties; it shall hold regular sessions every two years, and may also hold

special sessions whenever this Treaty so provides or, in the opinion of the Council, the circumstances so require.

2.   The General Conference:

(a) May consider and decide on any matters or questions covered by this Treaty, within the limits thereof, including those referring to powers and functions of any organ provided for in this Treaty.

(b) Shall establish procedures for the control system to ensure observance of this Treaty in accordance with its provisions.

(c) Shall elect the Members of the Council and the General Secretary.

(d) May remove the General Secretary from office if the proper functioning of the Agency so requires.

(e) Shall receive and consider the biennial and special reports submitted by the Council and the General Secretary.

(f) Shall initiate and consider studies designed to facilitate the optimum fulfillment of the aims of this Treaty, without prejudice to the power of the General Secretary independently to carry out similar studies for submission to and consideration by the Conference.

(g) Shall be the organ competent to authorize the conclusion of agreements with Governments and other international organizations and bodies.

3.   The General Conference shall adopt the Agency's budget and fix the scale of financial contributions to be paid by Member States, taking into account the systems and criteria used for the same purpose by the United Nations.

4.   The General Conference shall elect its officers for each session and may establish such subsidiary organs as it deems necessary for the performance of its functions.

5.   Each Member of the Agency shall have one vote. The decisions of the General Conference shall be taken by a two-thirds majority of the Members present and voting in the case of matters relating to the control system and measures referred to in article 20, the admission of new Members, the election or removal of the General Secretary, adoption of the budget and matters related thereto. Decisions on other matters, as well as procedural questions and also determination of which questions must be decided by a two-thirds majority, shall be taken by a simple majority of the Members present and voting.

6.   The General Conference shall adopt its own rules of procedure.

The Council

Article 10

1.   The Council shall be composed of five Members of the Agency elected by the General Conference from among the Contracting Parties, due account being taken of equitable geographic distribution.

2.   The Members of the Council shall be elected for a term of four years. However, in the first election three will be elected for two years. Outgoing Members may not be re-elected for the following period unless the limited number of States for which the Treaty is in force so requires.

3.   Each Member of the Council shall have one representative.

4.   The Council shall be so organized as to be able to function continuously.

5.   In addition to the functions conferred upon it by this Treaty and to those which may be assigned to it by the General Conference, the Council shall, through the General Secretary, ensure the proper operation of the control system in accordance with the provisions of this Treaty and with the decisions adopted by the General Conference.

6.   The Council shall submit an annual report on its work to the General Conference as well as such special reports as it deems necessary or which the General Conference requests of it.

7.   The Council shall elect its officers for each session.

8.   The decisions of the Council shall be taken by a simple majority of its Members present and voting.

9.   The Council shall adopt its own rules of procedure.

The Secretariat

Article 11

1.   The Secretariat shall consist of a General Secretary, who shall be the chief administrative officer of the Agency, and of such staff as the Agency may require. The term of office of the General Secretary shall be four years and he may be re-elected for a single additional term. The General Secretary may not be a national of the country in which the Agency has its headquarters. In case the office of General Secretary becomes vacant, a new election shall be held to fill the office for the remainder of the term.

2.   The staff of the Secretariat shall be appointed by the General Secretary, in accordance with rules laid down by the General Conference.

3.   In addition to the functions conferred upon him by this Treaty and to those which may be assigned to him by the General Conference,—the General Secretary shall ensure, as provided by article 10, paragraph 5, the proper operation of the control system established by this Treaty, in accordance with the provisions of the Treaty and the decisions taken by the General Conference.

4.   The General Secretary shall act in that capacity in all meetings of the General Conference and of the Council and shall make an annual report to both bodies on the work of the Agency and any special reports requested by the General Conference or the Council or which the General Secretary may deem desirable.

5.   The General Secretary shall establish the procedures for distributing to all Contracting Parties information received by the Agency from governmental sources and such information from non-governmental sources as may be of interest to the Agency.

6.   In the performance of their duties the General Secretary and the staff shall not seek or receive instructions from any Government or from any other authority external to the Agency and shall refrain from any action which might reflect on their position as international officials responsible only to the Agency; subject to their responsibility to the Agency, they shall not disclose any industrial secrets or other confidential information coming to their knowledge by reason of their official duties in the Agency.

7.   Each of the Contracting Parties undertakes to respect the exclusively international character of the responsibilities of the General Secretary and the staff and not to seek to influence them in the discharge of their responsibilities.

Control system

Article 12

1.   For the purpose of verifying compliance with the obligations entered into by the Contracting Parties in accordance with article 1, a control system shall be established which shall be put into effect in accordance with the provisions of articles 13-18 of this Treaty.

2.   The control system shall be used in particular for the purpose of verifying:

(a) That devices, services and facilities intended for peaceful uses of nuclear energy are not used in the testing or manufacture of nuclear weapons,

(b) That none of the activities prohibited in article 1 of this Treaty are carried out in the territory of the Contracting Parties with nuclear materials or weapons introduced from abroad, and

(c) That explosions for peaceful purposes are compatible with article 18 of this Treaty.

IAEA safeguards

Article 13

Each Contracting Party shall negotiate multilateral or bilateral agreements with the International Atomic Energy Agency for the application of its safeguards to its nuclear activities. Each Contracting Party shall initiate negotiations within a period of 180 days after the date of the deposit of its instrument of ratification of this Treaty. These agreements shall enter into force, for each Party, not later than eighteen months after the date of the initiation of such negotiations except in case of unforeseen circumstances or *force majeure.*

Reports of the Parties

Article 14

1.   The Contracting Parties shall submit to the Agency and to the International Atomic Energy Agency, for their information, semi-annual reports stating that no activity prohibited under this Treaty has occurred in their respective territories.

2.   The Contracting Parties shall simultaneously transmit to the Agency a copy of any report they may submit to the International Atomic Energy Agency which relates to matters that are the subject of this Treaty and to the application of safeguards.

3.   The Contracting Parties shall also transmit to the Organization of American States, for its information, any reports that may be of interest to it, in accordance with the obligations established by the Inter-American System.

Special reports requested by the General Secretary

Article 15

1.   With the authorization of the Council, the General Secretary may request any of the Contracting Parties to provide the

Agency with complementary or supplementary information regarding any event or circumstance connected with compliance with this Treaty, explaining his reasons. The Contracting Parties undertake to co-operate promptly and fully with the General Secretary.

2.   The General Secretary shall inform the Council and the Contracting Parties forthwith of such requests and of the respective replies.

Special inspections

Article 16

1.   The International Atomic Energy Agency and the Council established by this Treaty have the power of carrying out special inspections in the following cases:

(a) In the case of the International Atomic Energy Agency, in accordance with the agreements referred to in article 13 of this Treaty;

(b) In the case of the Council:

(i) When so requested, the reasons for the request being stated, by any Party which suspects that some activity prohibited by this Treaty has been carried out or is about to be carried out, either in the territory of any other Party or in any other place on such latter Party's behalf, the Council shall immediately arrange for such an inspection in accordance with article 10, paragraph 5.

(ii) When requested by any Party which has been suspected of or charged with having violated this Treaty, the Council shall immediately arrange for the special inspection requested in accordance with article 10, paragraph 5.

The above requests will be made to the Council through the General Secretary.

2.   The costs and expenses of any special inspection carried out under paragraph 1, sub-paragraph (b), sections (i) and (ii) of this article shall be borne by the requesting Party or Parties, except where the Council concludes on the basis of the report on the special inspection that, in view of the circumstances existing in the case, such costs and expenses should be borne by the Agency.

3.   The General Conference shall formulate the procedures for the organization and execution of the special inspections carried out in accordance with paragraph 1, sub-paragraph (b), sections (i) and (ii) of this article.

4.   The Contracting Parties undertake to grant the inspectors carrying out such special inspections full and free access to all places and all information which may be necessary for

the performance of their duties and which are directly and intimately connected with the suspicion of violation of this Treaty. If so requested by the authorities of the Contracting Party in whose territory the inspection is carried out, the inspectors designated by the General Conference shall be accompanied by representatives of said authorities, provided that this does not in any way delay or hinder the work of the inspectors.

5. The Council shall immediately transmit to all the Parties, through the General Secretary, a copy of any report resulting from special inspections.

6. Similarly, the Council shall send through the General Secretary to the Secretary-General of the United Nations, for transmission to the United Nations Security Council and General Assembly, and to the Council of the Organization of American States, for its information, a copy of any report resulting from any special inspection carried out in accordance with paragraph 1, sub-paragraph (b), sections (i) and (ii) of this article.

7. The Council may decide, or any Contracting Party may request, the convening of a special session of the General Conference for the purpose of considering the reports resulting from any special inspection. In such a case, the General Secretary shall take immediate steps to convene the special session requested.

8. The General Conference, convened in special session under this article, may make recommendations to the Contracting Parties and submit reports to the Secretary-General of the United Nations to be transmitted to the United Nations Security Council and the General Assembly.

Use of nuclear energy for peaceful purposes

Article 17

Nothing in the provisions of this Treaty shall prejudice the rights of the Contracting Parties, in conformity with this Treaty, to use nuclear energy for peaceful purposes, in particular for their economic development and social progress.

Explosions for peaceful purposes

Article 18

1. The Contracting Parties may carry out explosions of nuclear devices for peaceful purposes—including explosions which involve devices similar to those used in nuclear weapons—or collaborate with third parties for the same purpose, provided that they do so in accordance with the provisions of

this article and the other articles of the Treaty, particularly articles 1 and 5.

2. Contracting Parties intending to carry out, or to cooperate in carrying out, such an explosion shall notify the Agency and the International Atomic Energy Agency, as far in advance as the circumstances require, of the date of the explosion and shall at the same time provide the following information:

(a) The nature of the nuclear device and the source from which it was obtained,

(b) The place and purpose of the planned explosion,

(c) The procedures which will be followed in order to comply with paragraph 3 of this article,

(d) The expected force of the device, and

(e) The fullest possible information on any possible radioactive fall-out that may result from the explosion or explosions, and measures which will be taken to avoid danger to the population, flora, fauna and territories of any other Party or Parties.

3. The General Secretary and the technical personnel designated by the Council and the International Atomic Energy Agency may observe all the preparations, including the explosion of the device, and shall have unrestricted access to any area in the vicinity of the site of the explosion in order to ascertain whether the device and the procedures followed during the explosion are in conformity with the information supplied under paragraph 2 of this article and the other provisions of this Treaty.

4. The Contracting Parties may accept the collaboration of third parties for the purpose set forth in paragraph 1 of the present article, in accordance with paragraphs 2 and 3 thereof.

Relations with other international organizations

Article 19

1. The Agency may conclude such agreements with the International Atomic Energy Agency as are authorized by the General Conference and as it considers likely to facilitate the efficient operation of the control system established by this Treaty.

2. The Agency may also enter into relations with any international organization or body, especially any which may be established in the future to supervise disarmament or measures for the control of armaments in any part of the world.

3. The Contracting Parties may, if they see fit, request the advice of the Inter-American Nuclear Energy Commission on

all technical matters connected with the application of this Treaty with which the Commission is competent to deal under its Statute.

Measures in the event of violation of the Treaty

Article 20

1. The General Conference shall take note of all cases in which, in its opinion, any Contracting Party is not complying fully with its obligations under this Treaty and shall draw the matter to the attention of the Party concerned, making such recommendations as it deems appropriate.

2. If, in its opinion, such non-compliance constitutes a violation of this Treaty which might endanger peace and security, the General Conference shall report thereon simultaneously to the United Nations Security Council and the General Assembly through the Secretary-General of the United Nations, and to the Council of the Organization of American States. The General Conference shall likewise report to the International Atomic Energy Agency for such purposes as are relevant in accordance with its Statute.

United Nations and Organization of American States

Article 21

None of the provisions of this Treaty shall be construed as impairing the rights and obligations of the Parties under the Charter of the United Nations or, in the case of States Members of the Organization of American States, under existing regional treaties.

Privileges and immunities

Article 22

1. The Agency shall enjoy in the territory of each of the Contracting Parties such legal capacity and such privileges and immunities as may be necessary for the exercise of its functions and the fulfillment of its purposes.

2. Representatives of the Contracting Parties accredited to the Agency and officials of the Agency shall similarly enjoy such privileges and immunities as are necessary for the performance of their functions.

3. The Agency may conclude agreements with the Contracting Parties with a view to determining the details of the application of paragraphs 1 and 2 of this article.

Notification of other agreements

Article 23

Once this Treaty has entered into force, the Secretariat shall be notified immediately of any international agreement concluded by any of the Contracting Parties on matters with which this Treaty is concerned; the Secretariat shall register it and notify the other Contracting Parties.

Settlement of disputes

Article 24

Unless the Parties concerned agree on another mode of peaceful settlement, any question or dispute concerning the interpretation or application of this Treaty which is not settled shall be referred to the International Court of Justice with the prior consent of the Parties to the controversy.

Signature

Article 25

1.   This Treaty shall be open indefinitely for signature by:
   (a) All the Latin American Republics, and
   (b) All other sovereign States situated in their entirety south of latitude 35° north in the western hemisphere; and, except as provided in paragraph 2 of this article, all such States which become sovereign, when they have been admitted by the General Conference.

2.   The General Conference shall not take any decision regarding the admission of a political entity part or all of whose territory is the subject, prior to the date when this Treaty is opened for signature, of a dispute or claim between an extracontinental country and one or more Latin American States, so long as the dispute has not been settled by peaceful means.

Ratification and deposit

Article 26

1.   This Treaty shall be subject to ratification by signatory States in accordance with their respective constitutional procedures.

2.   This Treaty and the instruments of ratification shall be deposited with the Government of the Mexican United States, which is hereby designated the Depositary Government.

3.   The Depositary Government shall send certified copies of this Treaty to the Governments of signatory States and shall notify them of the deposit of each instrument of ratification.

Reservations

Article 27

This Treaty shall not be subject to reservations.

Entry into force

Article 28

1.   Subject to the provisions of paragraph 2 of this article, this Treaty shall enter into force among the States that have ratified it as soon as the following requirements have been met:

(a) Deposit of the instruments of ratification of this Treaty with the Depositary Government by the Governments of the States mentioned in article 25 which are in existence on the date when this Treaty is opened for signature and which are not affected by the provisions of article 25, paragraph 2;

(b) Signature and ratification of Additional Protocol I annexed to this Treaty by all extra-continental or continental States having *de jure* or *de facto* international responsibility for territories situated in the zone of application of the Treaty;

(c) Signature and ratification of the Additional Protocol II annexed to this Treaty by all powers possessing nuclear weapons;

(d) Conclusion of bilateral or multilateral agreements on the application of the Safeguards System of the International Atomic Energy Agency in accordance with article 13 of this Treaty.

2.   All signatory States shall have the imprescriptible right to waive, wholly or in part, the requirements laid down in the preceding paragraph. They may do so by means of a declaration which shall be annexed to their respective instrument of ratification and which may be formulated at the time of deposit of the instrument or subsequently. For those States which exercise this right, this Treaty shall enter into force upon deposit of the declaration, or as soon as those requirements have been met which have not been expressly waived.

3.   As soon as this Treaty has entered into force in accordance with the provisions of paragraph 2 for eleven States, the Depositary Government shall convene a preliminary meeting of those States in order that the Agency may be set up and commence its work.

4.   After the entry into force of this Treaty for all the countries of the zone, the rise of a new power possessing nuclear weapons shall have the effect of suspending the execution of this Treaty for those countries which have ratified it without waiving requirements of paragraph 1, sub-paragraph (c) of this article, and which request such suspension; the Treaty shall remain suspended until the new power, on its own

initiative or upon request by the General Conference, ratifies the annexed Additional Protocol II.

Amendments

Article 29

1.   Any Contracting Party may propose amendments to this Treaty and shall submit its proposals to the Council through the General Secretary, who shall transmit them to all the other Contracting Parties and, in addition, to all other signatories in accordance with article 6. The Council, through the General Secretary, shall immediately following the meeting of signatories convene a special session of the General Conference to examine the proposals made, for the adoption of which a two-thirds majority of the Contracting Parties present and voting shall be required.

2.   Amendments adopted shall enter into force as soon as the requirements set forth in article 28 of this Treaty have been complied with.

Duration and denunciation

Article 30

1.   This Treaty shall be of a permanent nature and shall remain in force indefinitely, but any Party may denounce it by notifying the General Secretary of the Agency if, in the opinion of the denouncing State, there have arisen or may arise circumstances connected with the content of this Treaty or of the annexed Additional Protocols I and II which affect its supreme interests or the peace and security of one or more Contracting Parties.

2.   The denunciation shall take effect three months after the delivery to the General Secretary of the Agency of the notification by the Government of the signatory State concerned. The General Secretary shall immediately communicate such notification to the other Contracting Parties and to the Secretary-General of the United Nations for the information of the United Nations Security Council and the General Assembly. He shall also communicate it to the Secretary-General of the Organization of American States.

Authentic texts and registration

Article 31

This Treaty, of which the Spanish, Chinese, English, French, Portuguese and Russian texts are equally authentic, shall be registered by the Depositary Government in accordance with article 102 of the United Nations Charter. The Depositary

Government shall notify the Secretary-General of the United Nations of the signatures, ratifications and amendments relating to this Treaty and shall communicate them to the Secretary-General of the Organization of American States for its information.

Transitional Article

Denunciation of the declaration referred to in article 28, paragraph 2, shall be subject to the same procedures as the denunciation of this Treaty, except that it will take effect on the date of delivery of the respective notification.

In witness whereof the undersigned Plenipotentiaries, having deposited their full powers, found in good and due form, sign this Treaty on behalf of their respective Governments.

Done at Mexico, Distrito Federal, on the Fourteenth day of February, one thousand nine hundred and sixty-seven.

ADDITIONAL PROTOCOL I

The undersigned Plenipotentiaries, furnished with full powers by their respective Governments,

Convinced that the Treaty for the Prohibition of Nuclear Weapons in Latin America, negotiated and signed in accordance with the recommendations of the General Assembly of the United Nations in Resolution 1911 (XVIII) of 27 November 1963, represents an important step towards ensuring the non-proliferation of nuclear weapons,

Aware that the non-proliferation of nuclear weapons is not an end in itself but, rather, a means of achieving general and complete disarmament at a later stage, and

Desiring to contribute, so far as lies in their power, towards ending the armaments race, especially in the field of nuclear weapons, and towards strengthening a world at peace, based on mutual respect and sovereign equality of States,

Have agreed as follows:

Article 1. To undertake to apply the statute of denuclearization in respect of warlike purposes as defined in articles 1, 3, 5 and 13 of the Treaty for the Prohibition of Nuclear Weapons in Latin America in territories for which, *de jure* or *de facto*, they are internationally responsible and which lie within the limits of the geographical zone established in that Treaty.

Article 2. The duration of this Protocol shall be the same as that of the Treaty for the Prohibition of Nuclear Weapons in Latin America of which this Protocol is an annex, and the provisions regarding ratification and denunciation contained in the Treaty shall be applicable to it.

Article 3. This Protocol shall enter into force, for the States which have ratified it, on the date of the deposit of their respective instruments of ratification.

In witness whereof the undersigned Plenipotentiaries, having deposited their full powers, found in good and due form, sign this Protocol on behalf of their respective Governments.

ADDITIONAL PROTOCOL II

The undersigned Plenipotentiaries, furnished with full powers by their respective Governments,

Convinced that the Treaty for the Prohibition of Nuclear Weapons in Latin America, negotiated and signed in accordance with the recommendations of the General Assembly of the United Nations in Resolution 1911 (XVIII) of 27 November

1963, represents an important step towards ensuring the non-proliferation of nuclear weapons,

Aware that the non-proliferation of nuclear weapons is not an end in itself but, rather, a means of achieving general and complete disarmament at a later stage, and

Desiring to contribute, so far as lies in their power, towards ending the armaments race, especially in the field of nuclear weapons, and towards promoting and strengthening a world at peace, based on mutual respect and sovereign equality of States,

Have agreed as follows:

Article 1. The statute of denuclearization of Latin America in respect of warlike purposes, as defined, delimited and set forth in the Treaty for the Prohibition of Nuclear Weapons in Latin America of which this instrument is an annex, shall be fully respected by the Parties to this Protocol in all its express aims and provisions.

Article 2. The Governments represented by the undersigned Plenipotentiaries undertake, therefore, not to contribute in any way to the performance of acts involving a violation of the obligations of article 1 of the Treaty in the territories to which the Treaty applies in accordance with article 4 thereof.

Article 3. The Governments represented by the undersigned Plenipotentiaries also undertake not to use or threaten to use nuclear weapons against the Contracting Parties of the Treaty for the Prohibition of Nuclear Weapons in Latin America.

Article 4. The duration of this Protocol shall be the same as that of the Treaty for the Prohibition of Nuclear Weapons in Latin America of which this Protocol is an annex, and the definitions of territory and nuclear weapons set forth in articles 3 and 5 of the Treaty shall be applicable to this Protocol, as well as the provisions regarding ratification, reservations, denunciation, authentic texts and registration contained in articles 26, 27, 30 and 31 of the Treaty.

Article 5. This Protocol shall enter into force, for the States which have ratified it, on the date of the deposit of their respective instruments of ratification.

In witness whereof, the undersigned Plenipotentiaries, having deposited their full powers, found to be in good and due form, hereby sign this Additional Protocol on behalf of their respective Governments.

Treaty for the Prohibition of Nuclear Weapons in Latin America

Country	Date of Signature	Date of Deposit of Ratification
Argentina	9/27/67	
Bahamas, The		7/16/76*
Barbados	10/18/68	4/25/69
Bolivia	2/14/67	2/18/69
Brazil	5/ 9/67	1/29/68†
Chile	2/14/67	10/ 9/74
Colombia	2/14/67	8/ 4/72
Costa Rica	2/14/67	8/25/69
Dominican Republic	7/29/67	6/14/68
Ecuador	2/14/67	2/11/69
El Salvador	2/14/67	4/22/68
Grenada	4/29/75	6/20/75
Guatemala	2/14/67	2/ 6/70
Haiti	2/14/67	5/23/69
Honduras	2/14/67	9/23/68
Jamaica	10/26/67	6/26/69
Mexico	2/14/67	9/20/67
Nicaragua	2/15/67	10/24/68
Panama	2/14/67	6/11/71
Paraguay	4/26/67	3/19/69
Peru	2/14/67	3/ 4/69
Surinam	2/13/76	
Trinidad & Tobago	6/27/67	12/ 3/70
Uruguay	2/14/67	8/20/68
Venezuela	2/14/67	3/23/70
Total	24	21

†Not in force. No declaration of waiver under Art. 28, para. 2.
*Succession

Appendix V

RESOLUTION 3472 B (XXX)
ON "COMPREHENSIVE STUDY OF THE QUESTION OF NUCLEAR-WEAPON-FREE ZONES IN ALL ITS ASPECTS" ADOPTED BY THE U.N. GENERAL ASSEMBLY ON DECEMBER 11, 1975

The General Assembly,

Recalling that, as set forth in the Charter of the United Nations, the Organization is based on the principle of the sovereign equality of all its Members and that, in conformity with the provisions of the Charter, international relations should be governed, among other fundamental principles, by those relating to the prohibition of the threat or use of force and to non-intervention,

Bearing in mind that nuclear-weapon-free zones constitute one of the most effective means for preventing the proliferation, both horizontal and vertical, of nuclear weapons and for contributing to the elimination of the danger of a nuclear holocaust,

Reaffirming the principle defined in its resolution 2028 (XX) of 19 November 1965, which established the necessity that there should be an acceptable balance of mutual responsibilities and obligations of the nuclear-weapon and non-nuclear-weapon States,

Reaffirming also the request made in its resolution 2153 A (XXI) of 17 November 1966 to all nuclear-weapon States to refrain from the use, or threat of use, of nuclear weapons against States which conclude regional treaties in order to ensure the total absence of nuclear weapons in their respective territories,

Having examined the comprehensive study of the question of nuclear-weapon-free zones in all its aspects carried out under the auspices of the Conference of the Committee on Disarmament by the Ad Hoc Group of the Qualified Governmental Experts for the Study of the Question of Nuclear-Weapon-Free Zones in pursuance of General Assembly resolution 3261 F (XXIX) of 9 December, 1974,

Having also examined the comments made by States members of the Conference of the Committee on Disarmament regarding that study, the text of which is annexed to the special report in which the Conference transmitted the study to the General Assembly,

Bearing in mind that, without prejudice to the results that may be obtained through any further examination of this matter, from the analysis of the contents of the special report it is already possible at this time to draw certain incontrovertible conclusions,

Noting that from among those conclusions it would seem advisable to stress the necessity that the General Assembly define the concept of a nuclear-weapon-free zone and the scope of the principal obligations of the nuclear-weapon States toward such zones and towards the States included therein,

Convinced that in so doing it will strengthen the new efforts recently undertaken and the realizations already achieved for the establishment of nuclear-weapon-free zones,

Solemnly adopts the following declaration:

I. Definition of the concept of a nuclear-weapon-free zone

1. A "nuclear-weapon-free zone" shall, as a general rule, be deemed to be any zone, recognized as such by the General Assembly of the United Nations, which any group of States, in the free exercise of their sovereignty, has established by virtue of a treaty or convention whereby:

   (a) The statue of total absence of nuclear weapons to which the zone shall be subject, including the procedure for the delimitation of the zone, is defined;

   (b) An international system of verification and control is established to guarantee compliance with the obligations deriving from that statute.

II. Definition of the principal obligations of the nuclear-weapon States toward nuclear-weapon-free zones and towards the States included therein

2. In every case of a nuclear-weapon-free zone that has been recognized as such by the General Assembly, all nuclear-weapon States shall undertake or reaffirm, in a solemn international instrument, having full legally binding force, such as a treaty, a convention, or a protocol, the following obligations:

   (a) To respect in all its parts the statute of total absence of nuclear weapons defined in the treaty or convention which serves as the constitutive instrument of the zone;

(b) To refrain from contributing in any way to the performance in the territories forming part of the zone of acts which involve a violation of the aforesaid treaty or convention;

(c) To refrain from using or threatening to use nuclear weapons against the States included in the zone.

III.   Scope of the definitions

3. The above definitions in no way impair the resolutions which the General Assembly has adopted or may adopt with regard to specific cases of nuclear-weapon-free zones nor the rights emanating for the Member States from such resolutions.

Appendix VI

Text of the Statement on Conventional Arms Transfer Policy

Issued by President Carter on May 19, 1977

The virtually unrestrained spread of conventional weaponry threatens stability in every region of the world. Total arms sales in recent years have risen to over $20 billion, and the United States accounts for more than one-half of this amount. Each year, the weapons transferred are not only more numerous, but also more sophisticated and deadly. Because of the threat to world peace embodied in this spiralling arms traffic; and because of the special responsibilities we bear as the largest arms seller, I believe that the United States must take steps to restrain its arms transfers.

Therefore, shortly after my Inauguration, I directed a comprehensive review of U.S. conventional arms transfer policy, including all military, political, and economic factors. After reviewing the results of this study, and discussing those results with members of Congress and foreign leaders, I have concluded that the United States will henceforth view arms transfers as an exceptional foreign policy implement, to be used only in instances where it can be clearly demonstrated that the transfer contributes to our national security interests. We will continue to utilize arms transfers to promote our security and the security of our close friends. But, in the future, the burden of persuasion will be on those who favor a particular arms sale, rather than those who oppose it.

To implement a policy of arms restraint, I am establishing the following set of controls, applicable to all transfers except those to countries with which we have major defense treaties (NATO, Japan, Australia, and New Zealand). We will remain faithful to our treaty obligations, and will honor our historic responsibilities to assure the security of the State of Israel. These controls will be binding unless extraordinary circumstances necessitate a Presidential exception, or where I determine that countries friendly to the United States must depend on advanced weaponry to offset quantitative and other disadvantages in order to maintain a regional balance.

1. The dollar volume (in constant Fiscal Year 1976 dollars) of

new commitments under the Foreign Military Sales and Military Assistance Programs for weapons and weapons-related items in Fiscal Year 1978 will be reduced from the Fiscal Year 1977 total. Transfers which can clearly be classified as services are not covered, nor are commercial sales, which the U.S. Government monitors through the issuance of export licenses. Commercial sales are already significantly restrained by existing legislation and Executive Branch policy.

2. The United States will not be the first supplier to introduce into a region newly-developed, advanced weapons systems which could create a new or significantly higher combat capability. Also, any commitment for sale or coproduction of such weapons is prohibited until they are operationally deployed with U.S. forces, thus removing the incentive to promote foreign sales in an effort to lower unit costs for Defense Department procurement.

3. Development or significant modification of advanced weapons systems solely for export will not be permitted.

4. Coproduction agreements for significant weapons, equipment, and major components (beyond assembly of subcomponents and the fabrication of high-turnover spare parts) are prohibited. A limited class of items will be considered for coproduction arrangements, but with restrictions on third-country exports, since these arrangements are intended primarily for the coproducer's requirements.

5. In addition to existing requirements of the law, the United States, as a condition of sale for certain weapons, equipment, or major components, may stipulate that we will not entertain any requests for retransfers. By establishing at the outset that the United States will not entertain such requests, we can avoid unnecessary bilateral friction caused by later denials.

6. An amendment to the International Traffic in Arms Regulations will be issued, requiring policy level authorization by the Department of State for actions by agents of the United States or private manufacturers, which might promote the sale of arms abroad. In addition, embassies and military representatives abroad will not promote the sale of arms and the Secretary of Defense will continue his review of government procedures, particularly procurement regulations, which may provide incentives for foreign sales.

In formulating security assistance programs consistent with these controls, we will continue our efforts to promote and advance respect for human rights in recipient countries. Also, we will assess the economic impact of arms transfers to those less-developed countries receiving U.S. economic assistance.

I am initiating this policy of restraint in the full understanding that actual reductions in the worldwide traffic in arms will require multilateral cooperation. Because we dominate the world market to such a degree, I believe that the United States can, and should, take the first step. However, in the immediate future, the United States will meet with other arms suppliers, including the Soviet Union, to begin discussions of possible measures for multilateral action. In addition, we will do whatever we can to encourage regional agreements among purchasers to limit arms imports.

Bibliography

In selecting works for further reading in arms control and disarmament issues, there is a strong temptation to bypass the vast body of literature produced since 1945 and recommend one or two timeless classics. For, while no one can deny that nuclear weapons have changed the world by making possible sudden annihilation against which there is no defense, there is much in both domestic and international politics which remains unchanged. Our preoccupation with the awesome power of nuclear weapons should not blind us to the lessons to be learned from pre-nuclear efforts to limit armaments as well as from pre-nuclear theories of what motivates the resort to armed conflict.

No nuclear-age stategist, for instance, has analyzed the theories of defense, deterrence and limited war more rigorously than did Thucydides 2,400 years ago in his history, *The Peloponnesian War.* Nor has any contemporary student or practitioner of arms control diplomacy produced a work to match Salvador de Madariaga's *Disarmament,* published in 1929. Consider the current relevance of the following passage, which describes the early League of Nations disarmament efforts but identifies one of the most troublesome problems inherent in pursuit of any formal agreement attempting to adjust military force levels:

> In the absence of a definite agreement implying reciprocal obligations, each state feels itself free to maintain a force which is a compromise between the ambitions of its fighting departments and the sobering influences of its exchequer. This internal compromise is relatively easy because there is a free future in which to revise it. If and when a definite engagement of an international, solemn and binding character, is envisaged, such a freedom threatens to vanish and then three sets of forces come into play, all tending to increase the figure to be "offered"; the tendency to reserve a margin against possible contingencies in international negotiation; prestige; and the necessity to provide a margin for discussion with the national exchequer. Such is the explanation of the warning often heard in League disarmament discussions to the effect that a conference for the reduction of armaments may well result in all-round increases.*

How can we then take seriously the analysts who claim that "bargaining chips" were first employed in the Strategic Arms

*Salvador de Madariaga, *Disarmament* (New York: Coward, McCann and Geoghegan, Inc., 1929), p. 31.

Limitation Talks (SALT)? Madariaga also dealt with the difficulties of measuring and then trying to balance military forces, given the asymmetries of geography, political systems and industrial development; the problems of verifying any agreements concluded; and the risk of exacerbating international tensions by focusing on the military capabilities of potential adversaries — all familiar problems in our own day.

Thus, in this selective bibliography an attempt has been made to blend historical works with those dealing with contemporary issues. The focus is primarily on topics likely to come before the Special Session, which means that certain areas have been omitted; there are no works, for example, which specifically deal with regional security or European arms control.

The selection begins with documents designed to provide useful background information on the Special Session itself. These are followed by works which deal with the traditional approach to arms control and disarmament, i.e., the pursuit of formal, international agreements. The Hague Conferences of 1899 and 1907, the League of Nations and the U.N. disarmament efforts, as well as some of the more recent efforts, are all touched upon. No attempt has been made to treat the contemporary forums in any depth but rather to cover the range of problems common to the negotiating process.

Governments have sought arms control agreements historically for a variety of motives. After major conflicts, security was generally pursued through peace settlements imposed by the victors over the vanquished. Between wars, incentives for control have included greater civilian claims on national resources, the hope that economically-dictated cuts at home might be reciprocated by former or potential adversaries, and that lower force levels would then reduce the risk of armed conflict or the damage should war occur. Whatever else the rhetoric may suggest, the single overriding motive has been to try not to be left in a militarily disadvantageous position. Some these efforts: *The Pipe Dream of Peace, The Disarmament Illusion, The Game of Disarmament, A Farewell to Arms Control?* After many decades of intense diplomatic effort and a number of treaties there has been no real disarmament in the sense of reduced force levels.

One reason why there has not been more success is that the determinants of force acquisition, which fuel the international competition in arms, are not yet well understood. If there is a consensus on the range of factors involved, there is little agreement on their relative importance. Perceptions of threat, foreign policy goals, international action-reaction phenomena, the will to compete, domestic bureaucratic politics and the momentum of technology are all recognized as playing a role. Yet serious questions remain as to whether domestic factors predominate over international pressures, or whether bureau-cratic-politics models, developed in the United States, are generally applicable to different political systems. Until the nature and complexity of the development and procurement of armed forces are taken into account, prescriptions for force limitations will inevitably lack coherence. A section of the bibliography under the heading, Impediments to Arms Control, includes works which attempt to grapple with these problems.

Then follow selections which explore alternative approaches to disarmament in the form of efforts to impose national restraints in force planning and arms reductions by mutual example.

These are followed by books and articles which treat in more depth some of the topics which were raised in the Talloires working papers: nuclear testing, problems of proliferation, economic issues of disarmament and development, conventional arms trade and the monitoring of agreements.

Finally, a number of periodicals are suggested for those wishing to follow contemporary arms control and disarmament developments.

Jane M.O. Sharp

Background to the 1978 Special Session

UNITED NATIONS DOCUMENTS

U.N. Secretariat. *Disarmament Resolutions Adopted by the General Assembly.* A/AC. 197/29 May 5, 1977.

_____. *Existing Principles and Proposals for the Conduct of Disarmament Negotiations.* A/AC. 187/30 May 2, 1977.

_____. *Views of Member States on the agenda and all other relevant questions relating to the Special Session of the General Assembly devoted to Disarmament.* A/AC. 187/51 May 14, 1977.

_____. *Working Paper submitted by Sri Lanka in behalf of the Non-Aligned Group.* A/AC. 187/55 May 18, 1977.

_____. *Disarmament and Development: proposal for a United Nations Study. Denmark, Finland, Norway, Sweden: Working Paper.* A/AC. 187/80 August 31, 1977.

_____. *Report of the Preparatory Committee for the Special Session of the General Assembly devoted to Disarmament.* GAOR 32nd Session Supplement #41 (A/32/41) September 27, 1977.

U.N. Office of Public Information. *The United Nations and Disarmament 1945-1970.*

OTHER PUBLICATIONS
DEALING WITH THE SPECIAL SESSION

Stanley Foundation, Muscatine, Iowa. *UN Special Session on Disarmament.* Report of the 8th Annual Conference on UN procedures, May 1977.

_____. *Multilateral Disarmament and the Special Session.* Report of the 12th Conference on the UN of the Next Decade, June 1977.

_____. *Report of the Eighteenth Strategy for Peace Conference,* October 1977.

Homer Jack. *A Sheaf of Documents on Disarmament: Early Background Materials for the Special Session.* New York: WCRP, 777 UN Plaza, N.Y., N.Y. 10017.

_____. "The Special Session on Disarmament: The Non-Aligned Leadership." *Revue of International Affairs* (Belgrade) Vol. 28 #656-657, August 5-20, 1977.

The Pursuit of Formal International Agreements

John H. Barton and Lawrence D. Weiler. *International Arms Control: Issues and Agreements.* Stanford: Stanford University Press, 1976.

Bernard G. Bechhoefer. *Postwar Negotiations for Arms Control.* Washington, D.C.: The Brookings Institution, 1961.

Hedley Bull. *The Control of the Arms Race,* 2nd Edition. New York: Praeger, 1966.

Abram Chayes. "An Inquiry into the Workings of Arms Control Agreements." *Harvard Law Review* Vol. 85 #5, March 1972.

Paul Doty, Albert Carnesale and Michael Nacht. "The Race to Control Nuclear Arms." *Foreign Affairs,* October 1976.

Trevor Dupuy and Guy Hammarman, Editors. *A Documentary History of Arms Control and Disarmament.* New York: R.R. Bowker Co., 1973.

Adrian S. Fisher. "Arms Control, Disarmament and International Law." *Virginia Law Review* Vol. 51 #7, November 1964.

Henry W. Forbes. *The Strategy of Disarmament.* Washington, D.C.: Public Affairs Press, 1962.

C. L. Gibson. "The Hague Peace Conference of 1899." *Military Review,* January 1976.

P. Terrence Hopmann. "Internal and External Influences on Bargaining in Arms Control Negotiations: The Partial Test Ban" in Bruce Russet, Editor. *War, Peace and Numbers.* Beverly Hills: Sage Publications, Inc., 1972.

Fred Iklé. *How Nations Negotiate.* New York: Harper and Row, 1964.

Morton Kaplan, Editor. *SALT: Problems and Prospects.* Morristown, New Jersey: General Learning Press, 1974.

Betty G. Lall. "Mutual Deterrence: The Need for a Definition." *Bulletin of Atomic Scientists,* December 1977. (An approach to comprehensive disarmament based on the Foster Panel findings in 1961.)

Salvador de Madariaga. *Disarmament.* New York: Coward, McCann and Geoghegan, Inc., 1929.

Alva Myrdal. *The Game of Disarmament.* New York: Pantheon, 1976.

John Newhouse. *Cold Dawn: The Story of SALT.* New York: Holt, Rinehart and Winston, 1973.

George H. Quester. *Nuclear Diplomacy: The First 25 Years.* New York: Dunnellen Co., Inc., 1970.

George Rathjens, Abram Chayes and Jack Ruina. *Nuclear Arms Control Agreements: Process and Impact.* Washington, D.C.: Carnegie Endowment, 1974.

Chalmers Roberts. *The Nuclear Years.* New York: Praeger, 1970.

Jack Sawyer and Harold Guetzkow. "Bargaining and Negotiation in International Relations" in Herbert C. Kelman, Editor. *International Behavior.* New York: Holt, Rinehart and Winston, 1965.

Herbert Scoville, Jr. "The SALT Negotiations." *Scientific American,* August 1977.

Louis B. Sohn and Grenville Clarke. *World Peace Through World Law,* 2nd Edition. Cambridge, Massachusetts: Harvard University Press, 1960.

John W. Spannier and Joseph L. Nogee. *The Politics of Disarmament: A Study in Soviet-American Gamesmanship.* New York: Praeger, 1962.

Merze Tate. *The Disarmament Illusion: The Movement for a Limitation of Armaments to 1907.* New York: MacMillan, 1942.

_____. *The United States and Armaments.* Cambridge, Massachusetts: Harvard University Press, 1954.

United States Arms Control and Disarmament Agency. *Arms Control and Disarmament Agreements: Texts and History of Negotiations.* Washington, D.C., June 1977.

John Wheeler-Bennett. *The Pipe Dream of Peace.* New York: Howard Fertig, 1971.

Mason Willrich and John Rhinelander. *SALT: The Moscow Agreements and Beyond.* New York: Free Press, 1974.

Herbert F. York, Editor. *Arms Control: Readings From Scientific American.* San Francisco: W. H. Freeman and Co., 1973.

Elizabeth Young. *A Farewell to Arms Control?* Harmondsworth, U.K.: Penguin Books, 1972.

Impediments to Arms Control:
Force Acquisitions and Arms Race Dynamics

Graham T. Allison and Frederic A. Morris. "Armaments and Arms Control: Exploring the Determinants of Military Weapons." *Daedalus,* Summer 1975.

Robert J. Art and Kenneth L. Waltz, Editors. *The Use of Force: International Politics and Foreign Policy.* Boston: Little, Brown and Co., 1971.

Steven Baker. "Arms Transfers and Nuclear Proliferation." *Arms Control Today* Vol. 4 #2, April 1977.

Robert J. Bressler and Robert G. Gray. "The Bargaining Chip and SALT." *Political Science Quarterly* Vol. 92 #1, Spring 1977.

Richard Burt. "New Weapons Technologies: Debate and Direction." *Adelphi Paper #126* (IISS, London), Summer 1976. 1976.

_____. "Proliferation and the Spread of New Conventional Weapons Technology." *International Security* Vol. 1 #3, Winter 1977.

_____. "The Cruise Missile and Arms Control." *Survival,* January/February 1976.

Luther J. Carter. "Strategic Arms Limitation: Leveling up to Symmetry." *Science,* February 21, 1975.

Robert Coulam. "The Importance of the Beginning: Defense

Doctrine and the F-111 Fighter Bomber." *Public Policy,* Winter 1975.

S. J. Dudzinsky, Jr. and James Digby. "New Technology and Control of Conventional Arms." *International Security* Vol. 1 #4, Spring 1977.

Bernard T. Feld, Ted Greenwood, George W. Rathjens and Steven Weinberg, Editors. *Impact of New Technologies on the Arms Race.* Cambridge, Massachusetts: MIT Press, 1971.

Randall Forsberg. *Resources Devoted to Military Research and Development.* Stockholm: Almqvist and Wiksell, 1972.

Colin S. Gray. "How Does the Nuclear Arms Race Work?" *Conflict and Cooperation* #2, 1974.

_____. "Of Bargaining Chips and Building Blocks: Arms Control and Defense Policy." *International Journal* (Canada), Spring 1973.

Ted Greenwood. *Making the MIRV: A Study of Defense Decision Making.* Cambridge, Massachusetts: Ballinger, 1975.

Ted Greenwood and Michael Nacht. "The Nuclear Debate: Sense or Nonsense?" *Foreign Affairs,* July 1974.

Samuel P. Huntington. "Arms Races: Prerequisites and Results." *Public Policy* (Harvard University), 1958.

James Kurth. "Why We Buy the Weapons We Do." *Foreign Policy* #11, Summer 1973.

Frank Long and George W. Rathjens, Editors. *Arms, Defense Policy and Arms Control.* New York: W.W. Norton, 1976.

M. J. Peck and F. M. Scherer. *The Weapons Acquisition Process.* Boston: Harvard University Graduate School of Business Administration, 1962.

George W. Rathjens. "The Dynamics of the Arms Race." *Scientific American,* April 1969.

Alexander R. Vershbow. "The Cruise Missile: The End of Arms Control." *Foreign Affairs,* October 1976.

Kenneth L. Waltz. *Man, the State and War: A Theoretical Analysis.* New York: Columbia University Press, 1959.

Albert Wohlstetter. "Is There a Strategic Arms Race?" *Foreign Policy* #15, Summer 1974.

_____. "Rivals But No Race." *Foreign Policy* #16, Fall 1974.

Herbert F. York. *Race to Oblivion: A Participant's View of the Arms Race.* New York: Simon and Schuster, 1970.

National Restraints and Mutual Example

Leonard Beaton. *The Reform of Power.* New York: Viking Press, 1972.

P. M. S. Blackett, "Steps Towards Disarmament." *Scientific American,* April 1962.

Kenneth E. Boulding. *Conflict and Defense: A General Theory.* New York: Harper and Row, 1962.

David V. Edwards. *Arms Control in International Politics.* New York: Holt, Rinehart and Winston, 1969.

Amitai Etzioni. "The Kennedy Experiment," Chapter 4 of *Studies in Social Change.* New York: Holt, Rinehart and Winston, 1966.

Erich Fromm. "The Case for Unilateral Disarmament" in Donald G. Brennan, Editor. *Arms Control, Disarmament and National Security.* New York: George Braziller, 1961.

Jerome D. Frank. *Sanity and Survival.* New York: Random House, 1967.

David Linebaugh. "The Once and Future Thing? Was There One Brief Moment When Arms Reduction Came to Camelot?" *Foreign Affairs Newsletter* Vol. 2 #13, July 1, 1976. (Institute for International Policy, Washington, D.C.)

——————. "We Cut, You Cut." *New York Times,* October 5, 1976.

——————. "SALT: An Agenda for Carter?" *Arms Control Today* Vol. 7 #3, March 1977.

John McNaughton. "Arms Restraint in Military Decisions." *Journal of Conflict Resolution* Vol. 7, September 1963.

Charles E. Osgood. *An Alternative to War and Surrender.* Urbana: University of Illinois Press, 1962.

M. Pilisuk and P. Skolnick. "Inducing Trust: A Test of the Osgood Proposal." *Journal of Personality and Social Psychology* #8, 1968.

Earl C. Ravenal. "The Case for Unilateral Arms Control Initiatives." *World Issues* #3, June/July 1977.

Jeffrey Record. *United States Theater Nuclear Weapons in Europe: Issues and Choices.* Washington, D.C.: The Brookings Institution, 1974.

——————. "U.S. Tactical Nuclear Weapons in Europe: 7,000 Warheads in Search of a Rationale." *Arms Control Today* Vol. 4 #4, April 1974.

Thomas C. Schelling. "Reciprocal Measures for Arms Stabilization" in Brennan, *op. cit.*

Dieter Senghaas. "Arms Race by Arms Control." *Bulletin of Peace Proposals* #4, 1975.

Gordon L. Schull. "Unilateral Initiatives and Arms Control: Problems and Prospects." *Ohio Arms Control Study Group.* Columbus, Ohio: Mershon Center of the Ohio State University, 1977.

Marek Thee. "Arms Control, the Retreat from Disarmament, and the Search for Alternatives." *Journal of Peace Research* Vol. XIV #2, 1977.

Paul C. Warnke. "Apes on a Treadmill." *Foreign Policy* #18, Spring 1975.

R. Waterkamp. "The Policy of Mutual Example in the Approach to Disarmament." *Frankfurter Hefte* Vol. 20 #3, 1965.

Nuclear Testing

Edward Bullard. "The Detection of Underground Explosions." *Scientific American,* July 1966.

Samuel Glasstone. *The Effects of Nuclear Weapons.* Washington, D.C.: United States Atomic Energy Commission, April 1962.

Jozef Goldblat. "TTBT/PNET: Steps Towards a CTBT?" *Instant Research on Peace and Violence* (Tampere, Finland) Vol. VII #1, 1977.

Thomas A. Halsted. "Why No End to Nuclear Testing?" *Survival* Vol. XIX #2, March/April 1977.

H. K. Jacobson and E. Stein. *Diplomats, Scientists and Politicians: The United States and the Nuclear Test Ban Negotiations.* Ann Arbor: University of Michigan Press, 1966.

Henry R. Myers. "Extending the Nuclear Test Ban." *Scientific American,* January 1972.

Milo D. Nordyke. "A Review of Soviet Data on the Peaceful Uses of Nuclear Explosions." *Annals of Nuclear Energy* Vol. 2. Oxford: Penguin Books, 1975.

U.S. Congress. *To Promote Negotiations for a Comprehensive Test Ban Treaty.* Hearings before the Senate Foreign Relations Committee, Subcommittee on Arms Control, International Law and Organization. Washington, D.C.: Government Printing Office, May 1973.

Jerome B. Wiesner and Herbert F. York. "National Security

and the Nuclear Test Ban." *Scientific American,* October 1964.

IIerbert F. York. "The Great Test Ban Debate." *Scientific American,* November 1972.

Nuclear Proliferation Problems

Richard Betts. "Paranoids, Pygmies, Pariahs and Non-Proliferation." *Foreign Policy #26,* Spring 1977.

Lincoln P. Bloomfield. "Nuclear Spread and World Order." *Foreign Affairs,* July 1975.

Hedley Bull. "Re-thinking Non-Proliferation." *International Affairs* (London), April 1975.

William Epstein. *A Nuclear-Weapon-Free Zone for Africa?* Occasional Paper #13. Stanley Foundation, Muscatine, Iowa, 1977.

Richard A. Falk. "A World Order Problem." *International Security* Vol. 1 #3, Winter 1977.

Bertrand Goldschmidt. "A Historical Survey of Non-Proliferation Policies." *International Security* Vol. 1 #1, Summer 1977.

Margaret Gowing. *Britain and Atomic Energy.* London: MacMillan Co., 1964.

_____. *Independence and Deterrence.* London: MacMillan Co., 1974.

Ted Greenwood, George Rathjens and Jack Ruina. "Nuclear Power and Weapons Proliferation." *Adelphi Paper #131* (IISS, London), 1977.

Spurgeon Keeny, Jr., Editor. *Nuclear Power: Issues and Choices.* Cambridge, Massachusetts: Ballinger, 1977.

Amory B. Lovins. *Non-Nuclear Futures. The Case for an Ethical Energy Strategy.* Cambridge, Massachusetts: Ballinger, 1975.

_____. *World Energy Strategies.* Cambridge, Massachusetts: Ballinger, 1975.

_____. "Energy Strategy: The Road Not Taken." *Foreign Affairs,* October 1976.

John McPhee. *The Curve of Binding Energy.* New York: Farrar, Straus and Giroux, 1974.

Anne Marks, Editor. *NPT: Paradoxes and Problems.* Washington, D.C.: Arms Control Association, Carnegie Endowment, 1975.

H. Peter Metzger. *The Atomic Establishment.* New York: Simon and Schuster, 1972.

Walter C. Patterson. *Nuclear Power.* London: Pelican Books, 1976.

George H. Quester. *The Politics of Proliferation.* Baltimore: Johns Hopkins Press, 1973.

Thomas C. Schelling. "Who Will Have the Bomb?" *International Security* Vol. 1 #1.

Martin J. Sherwein. *A World Destroyed: The Atom and the Grand Alliance.* New York: Knopf, 1975.

Stockholm International Peace Research Institute. *Nuclear Proliferation Problems.* Stockholm: Almqvist and Wiksell, 1974.

United Nations. *Comprehensive Study of the Question of Nuclear Weapons Free Zones in All its Aspects. A/10027 Addendum #1.* New York: UN, 1975.

U.S. Congress. *Non-Proliferation Issues.* Hearings before the Senate Foreign Relations Committee, Subcommittee on Arms Control, International Law and Organization. 94th Congress, 1st and 2nd sessions, 1976.

_____. *Nuclear Reduction, Testing and Non-Proliferation.* Hearings before the Senate Foreign Relations Committee, Subcommittee on Arms Control, International Law and Organization, 94th Congress, 1st and 2nd sessions, 1976.

_____. *Nuclear Proliferation Fact Book.* A congressional research service report prepared for the House Committee on International Relations and the Senate Committee on Governmental Affairs, September 23, 1977.

Mason Willrich and Theodore Taylor. *Nuclear Theft: Risks and Safeguards.* Cambridge, Massachusetts: Ballinger, 1974.

Disarmament and Development: Economic Issues and the Conventional Arms Trade

J. Barton. "The Developing Nations and Arms Control." *Studies in Comparative International Development* #10, 1975.

Richard R. Baxter. "Conventional Weapons Under Legal Prohibition" *International Security* Vol. 1 #3, Winter 1977.

Emile Benoit. *Defense and Economic Growth in Developing Countries.* Lexington, Massachusetts: Heath, 1973.

Emile Benoit and Kenneth E. Boulding, Editors. "*Disarmament and the Economy.* New York: Harper and Row, 1963.

Anne H. Cahn, Joseph J. Kruzel, Peter M. Dawkins and Jacques Huntzinger. *Controlling Future Arms Trade.* New York: Council on Foreign Relations, December 1977.

Richard A. Falk and Saul H. Mendlovitz, Editors. *Disarmament and Economic Development,* Volume IV of *The Strategy of World Order.* New York: World Law Fund, 1966.

Leslie Gelb. "Arms Sales." *Foreign Policy #25,* Winter 1976-1977.

Irving L. Horowitz. *Three Worlds of Development.* New York: Oxford University Press, 1966.

Mary Kaldor. "Military Technology and Social Structure." *Bulletin of the Atomic Scientists,* June 1977.

Betty G. Lall. *Prosperity Without Guns: The Economic Implications of Reductions in Defense Spending.* New York: Institute for World Order, November 1977.

Edward C. Luck. "The United Nations and the International Arms Trade" in David Kay, Editor. *The Changing UN: Options for the U.S.* Proceedings of the Academy of Political Science, November 1977.

Peter Lock and Herbert Wulf. *Register of Arms Production in Developing Countries.* Hamburg Study Group on Armaments and Underdevelopment, 1977.

Seymour Melman, Editor. *Disarmamemt: Its Politics and Economics.* Boston: American Academy of Arts and Sciences, 1962.

Bruce M. Russett. *What Price Vigilance? The Burdens of National Defense.* New Haven: Yale University Press, 1971.

Stockholm International Peace Research Institute. *Arms Trade With the Third World.* Stockholm: Almqvist and Wiksell, 1971.

Ruth L. Sivard. *World Military and Social Expenditures 1977.* Washington, D.C.: WMSE Publications, 1977.

Anthony Sampson. *The Arms Bazaar: From Lebanon to Lockheed.* New York: Viking, 1977.

George Thayer. *The War Business: The International Trade in Armaments.* New York: Avon, 1970.

Marek Thee. "Arms Trade and Transfer of Military Technology." *Bulletin of Peace Proposals* Vol. XIII #2, 1971.

U.N.A.-U.S.A. National Policy Panel. *Controlling the Conventional Arms Race.* New York: UNA, December 1976.

United Nations. *Disarmament and Development.* Report of the Group of Experts on the Economic and Social Consequences of Disarmament. ST/ECA/174, New York, 1972.

_____. *Reductions of the Military Budgets of State Permanent Members of the Security Council by 10% and Utilization of Part of the Funds Thus Saved to Provide Assistance to Developing Countries.* A/9770 New York, October 1974.

Monitoring Arms Control Agreements

Richard Dean Burns. "Supervision, Control and Inspection of Armaments: 1919-41 Perspective." *Orbis* Vol. XV #3, Fall 1971.

Richard A. Falk and Richard J. Barnet. *Security in Disarmament.* Princeton: Princeton University Press, 1965.

R. Gillette. "Nuclear Testing Violation. Keeping It All in the Family." *Science* #185, August 9, 1945.

Colin S. Gray. "SALT II Aftermath: Have the Soviets Been Cheating?" *Air Force Magazine* Vol. 58 #11, November 1975.

Ted Greenwood. "Reconnaissance, Surveillance and Arms Control." *Adelphi Paper #88* (IISS, London), 1972.

_____. "Reconnaissance and Arms Control." *Scientific American,* February 1973.

Institute for Defense Analyses. *Verification and Response in Disarmament Agreements. Report of the Woods Hole Summer Study.* Washington, D.C.: IDA, 1962.

Andrzej Karkoszka. *Strategic Disarmament, Verification and National Security.* London: Taylor and Francis, 1977. (A SIPRI publication.)

Jan M. Lodal. "Verifying SALT." *Foreign Policy* #24, Fall 1976.

George W. Rathjens. "The Verification of Arms Control Agreements." *Arms Control Today* Vol. 7 #7/8, July/August 1977.

U.S. Arms Control and Disarmament Agency. *Verification: The Crucial Element of Arms Control.* Washington, D.C.: ACDA, 1976.

Periodicals Dealing with Arms Control and Disarmament Issues

ANNUAL PUBLICATIONS

World Armaments and Disarmament. Stockholm International Peace Research Institute (SIPRI).

Military Balance. London: International Institute for Strategic Studies (IISS).

Strategic Survey. IISS.

Documents on Disarmament. Washington, D.C.: US Arms Control and Disarmament Agency (ACDA).

QUARTERLY JOURNALS

Aussenpolitik. Hamburg: West German Foreign Affairs Review.

Bulletin of Peace Proposals. Oslo: International Peace Research Institute.

Cooperation and Conflict. Oslo: Norwegian Institute of International Affairs.

International Security. Cambridge, Massachusetts: Harvard University, Program for Science and International Affairs.

Instant Research on Peace and Violence. Tampere, Finland: Tampere Peace Research Institute (TAPRI).

Journal of Conflict Resolution. Beverly Hills, California: Sage Publications.

Journal of Peace Research. Oslo: International Peace Research Institute.

BI-MONTHLY

Survival. IISS.

MONTHLY

Arms Control Today. Washington, D.C.: Arms Control Association.

Scientific American.

The Bulletin of the Atomic Scientists. Chicago, Illinois: The Educational Foundation for Nuclear Science.

Index

Middle East war of 1973, 47, 50
Myrdal, Alva, 52

NATO, 48, 50
Netherlands, 53-54
New Zealand, 53
Nigeria, 48, 53
Nixon Doctrine, 50
Non-Proliferation Treaty (NPT),
3, 14, 22-32, 60, 70, 72-73
Norway, 53
Nuclear Non-Proliferation Act
of 1977, 31
Nuclear-weapon-free zones, 35-43

OPANAL, 40-41
Outer Space Treaty, 70

Pacific, 35, 42
Pakistan, 24, 25, 51, 58
Pakistani wars, 63
Patton tanks, 63
Pechora-Kama Canal, 14
Peaceful nuclear explosions (PNE),
2, 3, 10-17, 27-28
PNE Treaty, 10, 13-14, 70
Persian Gulf, 47, 57
Peru, 51
Philippines, 50, 53
Preparatory Commission for the
Denuclearization of Latin
America (COPREDAL), 38-42

Rajaratnam, S., 53

Sadat, Anwar, 50
Saudi Arabia, 50, 58
Scandinavia, 35
Schlesinger, James, 21
Sea-Bed Treaty, 70
Shah of Iran, 49
Sinai Agreement of 1975, 49
Singapore, 53
Somalia, 58
South Africa, 55
South Asia, 48, 51
South Korea, 51, 58, 64
South-East Asia, 43
Spruance class destroyers, 48
Strategic Arms Limitations Talks
(SALT), 12, 20, 22, 23
Standing Consultative Committee,
12, 17, 75
Sudan, 58
Sub-Saharan Africa, 56
Suppliers Club, (London suppliers
group), 25, 29, 30

Sweden, 53

Tanzania, 51
Taiwan, 55
Third World, 41, 53-57, 61-66
Threshold Test Ban Treaty (TTBT),
3, 10, 14, 70
Treaty for the Prohibition of Nuclear
Weapons in Latin America (Treaty
of Tlatelolco), 4, 24, 36-43, 70, 72,
75
Additional Protocol I, 38
Additional Protocol II, 38, 41
contracting parties, 40
Turkey, 49

U Thant, 40
Union of Soviet Socialist
Republics (U.S.S.R.), 2, 4, 9-18,
22-23, 27-32, 49-50, 52, 54, 63
Mediterranean fleet, 50
United Kingdom, 2, 4, 10, 20, 47,
52-54
United Nations, 6, 9, 35, 37, 41,
52-54, 70-76
Annual Report, 7
Arms Review Committee, 8
Center for Disarmament, 76
Charter, 7, 36, 71
Eighteen Nation Committee on
Disarmament, 53
General Assembly, 1, 9, 12, 35-37,
41-42, 53-54
Security Council, 7, 41, 70-72
Special Session on Disarmament
(UNSSOD), 1-8, 17-18, 32, 61-66
United States, 2, 4, 9-11, 13, 16,
17-23, 27-32, 40, 47, 49-52, 54,
58-59, 62-66, 74
Congress, 31
Budget Office, 52
Senate, 10
Foreign Relations Committee, 10
Nevada test site, 11
Uruguay, 58

Vance, Cyrus, 10
Vietnam, 20, 62

Warsaw Pact, 48, 54
West Africa, 64
Western Europe, 25, 66
Western European Union, 75
Armaments Control Agency, 75
World War II, 62

Yugoslavia, 53